WHAT'S ANOTHER YEAR?

First published in 2016 by
Liberties Press
140 Terenure Road North | Terenure | Dublin 6W
T: +353 (1) 405 5701| www.libertiespress.com | E: info@libertiespress.com

Trade enquiries to Gill
Hume Avenue | Park West | Dublin 12
T: +353 (1) 500 9534 | F: +353 (1) 500 9595 | E: sales@gill.ie

Distributed in the United Kingdom by
Turnaround Publisher Services
Unit 3 | Olympia Trading Estate | Coburg Road | London N22 6TZ
T: +44 (0) 20 8829 3000 | E: orders@turnaround-uk.com

Distributed in the United States by
Casemate-IPM | 1950 Lawrence Road | Havertown, PA 19083
T: +1 (610) 853-9131 | E: casemate@casematepublishers.com

ISBN: 978-1-910742-43-3
2 4 6 8 10 9 7 5 3 1

A CIP record for this title is available from the British Library.

Cover design by Karen Vaughan
Internal design by Liberties Press

If you would like to contact the author with regards to corrections, copyright, omissions or
anything else regarding this book, please e-mail: whatsanotheryear@hotmail.com

WHAT'S ANOTHER YEAR?

IRELAND'S FIRST FIVE DECADES AT THE EUROVISION

MICK LYNCH

For Anna and Mikey

FOREWORD

BY SHAY HEALY

I was a member of the camera crew on the first-ever National Song Contest in RTÉ in 1965 and I've always had a sentimental spot for the Eurovision Song Contest. Since then there has been a plethora of books, magazine and newspaper articles, and radio and television documentaries that add up to an unquenchable desire for even more information. This handsome book is the icing on the cake, a celebration of the songs, and the singers who sang for Ireland, in the Eurovision Song Contest. The contest itself has emerged as Europe's Grand Dame, a musical extravaganza that is still growing.

The candid interviews and first-hand accounts with all the big players make this book special. Mick Lynch spins his stories into a strong narrative, full of tension, doubts and, of course, the unexpected. The book is a warm account of how Ireland fared over the past fifty years. Mick lets the people who were involved tell their own stories.

–Shay Healy

PREFACE

Walking out of Sunday-morning Mass in Mountmellick in April 1980, I caught a glimpse of the Sunday papers my granny and aunt would buy on a weekly basis from the guys selling them out of the back of a van. There on the front page was a headline proclaiming that Johnny Logan had won the Eurovision Song Contest for Ireland. This was the first time I'd heard the word 'Eurovision'; it marked the start of a lifetime of admiration for the event. The hosting of the contest in Dublin the following year made it even more important. Cathal Dunne's 'Happy Man' was the first Irish Eurovision song I became familiar with.

The very mention of the Eurovision Song Contest (ESC) brings out the cynics. Like it or loath it, we as a nation cheer on our entrant every year, hoping to restore a bit of Irish pride. Having not succeeded since 1996, it just goes to prove how hard it is to win it nowadays.

No one has won the contest more times than we have, so we have the right to be crowned champions of the Eurovision. Fionnuala Sherry, Phil Coulter and Mike Nolan have also had the luck of the Irish in this competition. Ireland could sum up its Eurovision history in three words: Logan, Gogan and Wogan. There are now many more names to add to that list. Lesser-known Irish people have been involved over the years, and all of them have as interesting a story to tell as the bigger names. With almost two hundred million watching in over forty countries, it's still as popular as ever. In 2015, Aimee Banks became our inaugural entrant in the Junior Eurovision Song Contest when she sang *Réalta na Mara* ('Star of the Sea') in Bulgaria, and this year Nicky Byrne goes to Stockholm with 'Sunlight', our fiftieth song representing Ireland at the Eurovision.

So why have we been so successful? What does it take to win ? Why has it proved more difficult in recent years? How do we win it again? I asked all the people who've been there, who've seen it first hand. From the backing singers, directors, producers, songwriters and singers, right up to the winning artists, they've all shared their memories of what we don't see on camera.

The Eurovision is more than just some cheesy songs and outrageous costumes. Behind it are many personal Irish stories of fun, sadness, laughter and heartache. It's also about friendships, break-ups and even marriages. This isn't a book that will bombard you with trivia. This is a first-hand, personal account, told by those that have a right to tell it. Some of it will shock and surprise you, but most of it will entertain you, because even the most ardent fan thinks they know the whole story; but what you see is only the final spectacle. 'Europe! Start reading now.'

–Mick Lynch
  County Laois

ACKNOWLEDGEMENTS

It takes more than the name of the author on the front of this book to put a piece of work like this together. It took endless e-mails, phone calls and any available social media to connect with all the people I wanted to interview for this project. From the moment I met Shay Healy, he thought it was a great idea, and was one hundred percent behind it in every way, providing me with various interviews and insights, and opening doors to numerous other people. I knew then that Shay was the man to write the foreword, and I'm honoured that he accepted.

All the following people have been supportive from the outset. In no particular order, I would like to thank each and every one of them for their contribution to this project: Linda Martin, Charlie McGettigan, the late Patricia O'Donnell, Muriel Day, Malcolm McDowell, Kim Jackson Grant, Brendan Graham, Paul Lyttle, Fionnuala Sherry, Rolf Lovland, Rune Andreassen, Signy and Tor Marne Jonassen, Maxi, Tommy and Jimmy Swarbrigg, Marc Roberts, Don Collins, Conor Mulhall, Tommy Nolan, Mickey Harte, Brian Kennedy, Bill Whelan, Johnny Logan, Dana, Christy Moore, Sandy Kelly, Donna McCaul, Niamh Kavanagh, Jackie Johnson, Dickie Rock, Rowland Soper, Paul Harrington, Liam Reilly, Eamonn Toal, Cathal Dunne, Eimear Quinn, Noel Curran, Aisling and Brendan Bowyer, Barry Devlin, Declan Lowney, Mike Nolan, Louis Walsh, John Kennedy O'Connor, Phil Coulter, Ian McGarry, Alma Carroll, Larry Gogan, Gay Byrne, Patricia Cahill, Martin McAloon, Leanne Moore, Michael Kealy, Seanin, Max and June Cunningham, Maria Christian, Bas Tukker, Francis Kennedy and Mary Kelehan.

To all the people in the media who have supported my work over the years, the Ian Dempsey Breakfast Show, Mairead Ronan and all at Today FM, The Ray Darcy Show including Jenny Kelly. Will Hanafin, Ryan Tubridy, Dave Fanning, and everyone at RTÉ Radio. John Clarke, Declan Meehan, Claire Darmody and East Coast FM, Ann Marie Kelly, Roy Jennings and Midlands 103, Betty Ryan and her late husband Ed, Tom Dunne and all at Newstalk, Alan Corr, John Pinder, *Hot Press*, Dick Doyle and Grainne Kavanagh at Irma, Phillipa Hayes at Chart-Track, Pat O Mahony, Phil Cawley, Shane Smyth, Garett Mulhall at Eurovision Ireland and everyone else who supported me last time round.

To my family, friends, workmates and relatives (too many to list here) who put up with my constant fascination with the Eurovision, including Pete Brennan, Rachel Grimes, Des and Mell Maguire, Kieran Murray, Mark Howard, Fergal and Noelle McGuirk, Andrew Basquille, Martin Daly, Damian Smyth, Jutta Bobbenkamp, and for all those I haven't name-checked, I apologise, but you know who you are.

Finally, this book is in honour of all the Irish men and women, both alive and deceased, who have been involved, and played their part, one way or another, in being ambassadors for their country over the past fifty years. and who haven't been afraid to take the knocks that came with it. Here's to the next fifty songs.

CONTENTS

CHAPTER ONE
THE NATIONAL SONG CONTEST

Long before Jennifer Lopez, the original J-Lo, Johnny Logan, was christened 'Mr Eurovision', some twenty-three broadcasting organisations formed the European Broadcasting Union (EBU) in 1950. Their objective was to cooperate with international broadcasts, and out of this would come the Eurovision, a way of exchanging TV programmes. At a meeting in 1955 Marcel Bezençon, the Director General of the Swiss Broadcasting Corporation, suggested a song contest similar to the San Remo festival that had been running in Italy. This time it would bring neighbouring countries together to compete. At a meeting in Rome later that year the idea was given the green light. It would be known as 'Eurovision Grand Prix', and Mr Bezençon got his wish to host it the following year.

The signature music that was played before all EBU broadcasts at the time was a piece called 'Te Deum', which had been written by French composer Marc-Antoine Charpentier in the seventeenth century. It was played to signify an EBU broadcast, and to this day can still be heard at the beginning and end of each Eurovision Song Contest.

On 24 May 1956, the first Eurovision Grand Prix was held in Lugano, Switzerland. It featured only seven countries, with each artist performing two songs on the night. Jetty Paerl from the Netherlands had the distinction of singing the very first song, but it was the host nation that took the prize, when Lys Assia performed her second song 'Refrain' and became the inaugural winner of the event.

Over the next ten years the contest's popularity grew, with new countries joining almost annually; the UK entered for the first time in 1957. Ireland would make its debut in the competition at the tenth Eurovision Grand Prix in Naples in 1965.

By the mid-sixties there was an abundance of musical talent in Ireland. The showband scene was booming, and acts like Brendan Bowyer and the Royal Showband, and Dickie Rock and the Miami, were filling dance halls up and down the country, so when it came to finding artists to sing a song in the National Song Contest there was no shortage of takers wanting to represent their country for the first time on the Eurovision stage.

The man responsible for the National Song Contest (NSC) in its early years, was the late Tom McGrath, a very popular man with everyone he worked with. He smoked a pipe, wore dark-rimmed glasses, and was a producer and director who had previously worked in Canada. Television was in its infancy at that time in Ireland. Television was his forte: he had the idea for *The Late Late Show* (from *The Tonight Show*), and became its first producer in 1962. He was given the responsibility of initiating the NSC, from which the winning song would represent Ireland in Italy. He won a Jacobs Award that year for his work. He was also the man who would offer the artist the song officially, and put the sound with the visuals; he became the Irish head of delegation at the Eurovision each year. He was a very down-to-earth kind of man and knew what the public wanted. Louis Walsh has fond memories of him:

> I remember Tom McGrath. He was very grumpy but he was right and he was always on it. He was a great producer and he cared, about the contest and about the act. He told us what to do, and he was great. We need another Tom Mc-Grath. He was brilliant.

For the inaugural NSC Tom had selected twelve songs and allocated one to each artist. The artists were Joan Connolly, Butch Moore, Patricia Cahill, Francis McDermott, the Jim Doherty Trio, John Keogh, Austin Gaffney, Amy Hayden, Terri Nerney, Paul Russell, Maisie McDaniel and Brendan Bowyer. Brendan sang 'Suddenly in Love' but was unhappy with his performance.

To be fair to the guy who wrote it, it was better than I gave it credit for. I was thinking, when it was all over, if I'd have treated it with a different tempo and done something with the song [it would have been better] but I just sang it off and I was disappointed in the way I did it. The song got a lot of criticism but I think I was responsible for not taking it seriously.

While some of the big names at that time in the Irish music scene were taking part, one high-profile singer was originally omitted from the inaugural event. Dickie Rock explains:

The song 'I Still Love You' was originally given to Maisie McDaniel. I didn't get a song. Maisie had an accident, and they came to my manager Tom Doherty, the manager of my band The Miami. By 1965 'Candy Store', 'There's Always Me' and 'I'm Yours' were all number one hits; I couldn't understand why I was overlooked for the song. They offered me the song that Maisie McDaniel sang. I said afterwards, maybe Maisie had the accident on purpose, because the song was brutal. That National Song Contest was a big deal in Ireland. In 1965, you had a huge number of showbands, and you're talking about 3,000 to 4,000 people at the dances in Cork. It was an amazing time and I got 'Suddenly in Love' in the National Song Contest. Butch Moore got 'Walking the Streets in the Rain', which he won with.

Butch became the winner that night, and Ireland finally took its place among the elite. Shay Healy was working for Radio Telefís Éireann (RTÉ).

I was a cameraman with RTÉ. I would have been working for the National Song Contest for Butch in 1965, as well as for Dickie in 1966. The station was only a few years old at this stage, and everybody rowed in. They pulled out all the stops for Butch Moore to put on the best show possible and not disgrace themselves in front of Europe. He finished sixth. I remember the homecoming for Butch. There was great excitement, and I always felt a bit of pride in it, and

that I owned a bit of the Eurovision, so when I came to
represent Ireland, it was like a long journey I'd been making
for over twenty years.

Only a small Irish delegation travelled to Naples in March 1965, as RTÉ was still a
relatively new television station and the finance wasn't there. Speaking with me in
1995, one of the songwriters, the late Teresa O Donnell (née Conlon), explained:

> We watched it from the green room in RTÉ as they couldn't
> afford to send us all out to Italy, but we were so proud of
> Butch's performance of our song.

While the honours that night went to the Serge Gainsbourg's composition *'Poupee
de Cire, Poupee de Son'*, it was Butch who made a lasting impression on one up-and-
coming Irish singer. Maxi recalls:

> I'd been interested in songs and songwriting forever, so I
> was a fan of Butch, though I was too young to go to the
> dances, but I wasn't too young to go to the airport with a
> placard. So I was just in a choir harmonising with Dick and
> Twink. I was too young to be let out at night, but not too
> young to watch the telly. My first memory of Butch was at
> the airport: I was with a whole gang of pals when Butch
> flew back and we waved and waved. I interviewed him years
> later, and worked with him in the United States. I later told
> him about that time and he said 'I know, I saw you clapping.'
> I knew that's what I wanted to do: I wanted to sing and be
> in the business

It had been an impressive debut, but Tom McGrath was adamant that Ireland could
do better. The following year he again selected twelve songs for the final, but this
time only opted for five acts. Surprisingly, Butch took part again, along with Deirdre
Wynne and The Ludlows, who were a popular group at the time with their single
'The Sea Around Us'. Sonny Knowles was another participant, and of his two songs,

'Chuaigh Me Suas Don Chluiche Mor' had the distinction of being the first Irish - language song to make the NSC final, and it would not be the last. Dickie returned, this time singing 'Can't Make Up My Mind', 'Oh Why' and 'Come Back To Stay', the latter a composition by Dublin singer Rowland Soper. Rowland was a good singer who never made it. Louis Walsh called him 'the one-hit wonder', but he had been resident at Cleary's Ballroom with Tommy O Brien, had been in the Metropole downstairs with Rory McGuinness and played various other venues over the years, including the Crystal Ballroom, Sundrive Road and the Apollo Cinemas. He also sang five nights a week on UTV doing a show called 'Teatime with Tommy', so he was already an established singer at that stage. Rowland explains the story behind the song:

I wrote that more or less for my wife. Her parents had a piano and you'd be waiting on your girlfriend and I'd be sitting messing with the piano. The daughter of variety-theatre guy Paddy Tyrell taught me four chords: C, A, F and G. I would play these, and there have been lots of things written about the song. People say 'Come Back To Stay' was supposed to have been copied from 'Unchained Melody', because if you listen to the words of both songs – 'Oh my love my darling, I hunger for your touch' and 'my love, I need your touch, I need your love' – you could arguably say that they're the same words, but there was no plagiarism. I learnt to play the four chords and I was a singer in variety shows all over Dublin. I sang 'Walk Away', a Matt Monro song, and that's C, A, F and G too, and I remember playing that, and just in the middle it became 'my love I need your touch, I need your love so very much', so they were the few songs I knew with C, A, F and G, and then I had my own one.

I had a school pal called Philip McNamara who is still my oldest friend. I wasn't the brightest student in the class, but he was good with a pen and he entered 'Come Back To Stay' for the National Song Contest, and funnily enough, I was a panel-beater, but at the time we were late with the entry. You got a form and we put down a *nom de plume*. We were late for the post, so I had to drive out to RTÉ that morning and go into the building's reception and hand it in on sheet music, as it was back then. A fellow called Jack Bayle scored it for me, as I can't write music, but then neither could Irving Berlin. When I asked Jack what he thought of it, he said 'It's a load of shite, so it'll probably win.' I sang the song and put it on a cassette; then Dickie came up to my mother-in-law's house and I recorded it for him. I played the piano and sang it. He got a copy of it, so it was exactly what I wanted.

'Come Back to Stay' won the NSC, and Rowland headed to Luxembourg with Dickie, Brendan O Reilly, Tom McGrath and Noel Kelehan, who was appearing at his first Eurovision. Dickie recalls:

We had a fantastic time. I'd never been to Luxembourg before. I wasn't really a social animal. I didn't drink or smoke. I went to rehearsals and then back to the hotel immediately to get ready. I always believed in having plenty of rest and eating good food when I'm going in for something, and I'll always make sure I'm well rested. I prepare well. You know what Roy Keane says: 'Fail to prepare, prepare to fail.' Rowland Soper was part of the RTÉ entourage. I hardly knew Rowland then, but we're great friends now.

Rowland also has fond memories of a fantastic experience:

I was from a tenement, twenty-five years of age, and the idea of hearing cowboys talking in a foreign language was a great thrill. It's usually the opposite when you live in Ireland. They were great times and we went to a lot of parties. Had Dickie won it, he was going straight on to *The Eamonn Andrews Sunday Night Show*. With all the parties afterwards, it felt a bit like the Oscars. Great memories. I recently found pictures of myself and Dickie at the airport heading out to the event.

Dickie remembers the competition on the night, and one artist in particular:

Domenico Modugno was in there that year too. He wrote so many great songs. He wrote *'Volare'*. The amazing thing about Domenico Modugno was that he was a big name, but what happened was that he caused a furore. Don't forget at that time, there was the singer, the orchestras and the song. There were no gimmicks, no dancers, no backing groups, but he wanted to have three people on the stage with him and there was an awful furore about the whole thing. Kenneth McKellar was probably wrong to wear his kilt. He was a fine singer, and a tenor. We always felt that, a few years later when I was doing cabaret in clubs or the Olympia, in Cork and around the country, when I'd matured more as a performer, if I had had that song we could have won it. I would have been able to sell the song better and my voice would have improved.

In old footage I'm standing with the microphone on the stand. That's unheard of. I have it in my hand and I'm moving around the stage. Even when I sing the song now, I sing it slightly differently, I sell the lyrics more. At that time I was using the hand microphone all over the stage, but barely had it in the stand. I don't know what the hell I was thinking. To think, three to four years later if I had got that song, it would have been a different ball game. I was disappointed to finish fourth, although it was great for our country. No matter what we do, the World Cup, Germany, everything, for our little country of four million, it was great to come joint fourth out of eighteen countries.

By 1967, Ireland was heading toward its third Eurovision, this time in Austria. Larry Gogan recalls how the contest was different that year.

The time that Sean Dunphy won, it was based on votes. I'm not sure if it was votes in the TV Guide. They say that Oliver Barry went all around town with these forms to fill in. It must have been *The RTÉ Guide*. The public had a right to vote that way. You filled in this form of who you wanted to sing this song.

While this voting system would benefit Sean, it was to have the opposite effect on the other participants. Unlike Sean, who only sang one song, Johnny McEvoy, Aedin Ni Choileain, Deidre O'Callaghan and Patricia Cahill all sang two. Patricia explains:

> I had two songs in that contest which, of course, split my vote. This was something nobody realised till after the votes started coming in, and my combined votes were higher than Sean's, who only had the one song. There was quite a to-do in the press, as you can imagine, and I did get the sympathy of the public. To be honest, I was so busy at that time – I was singing in *The Student Prince* and recording the songs I had sung – that I didn't really think about what had happened.
>
> I had always sung with my hair down. I had very long hair, and Tom McGrath, the producer of the show, suggested that I put it up for this show. What his reason for this was, I don't know, and never thought to ask, but the hair was up for the contest. The floors, I remember, were painted a lovely aquamarine. My dress happened to be the same colour, with a white lace top. That memory makes me smile! I'll never know whether my singing career would have been more successful as a result of the contest, but for me my career couldn't have turned out better. I have had a great career singing all over the world, and a wonderful personal life, so, no complaints or regrets. I remember getting a lot of letters from Vienna from people who had been expecting me to win. Fate played a hand, and Sean went off to Vienna.

Sean wasn't the only Irish representative in Vienna. He was up against an Irish songwriter who was just finding his craft. Phil Coulter had grown up in Derry and his first memories of the Eurovision were Pearl Carr and Teddy Johnson's 'Sing Little Birdie' in 1959. He had written 'Foolin' Time' for Butch Moore and The Capitol Showband, before Butch went to Naples, and by 1967, along with companion Bill Martin, he was a contracted songwriter for Keith Prowse Music in London. Based in Denmark Street, this was where the whole of the UK music publishing industry was concentrated. This was the engine room of British songwriting, including Greenaway and Cook, Murray and Callander, Graham Gouldman, Geoff Stephens, Les Reed and Barry Mason. Phil recalls how he wrote his first Eurovision song:

We'd had a few album tracks and a few minor hits, and our publisher comes around and says: 'Right boys, Eurovision time. The BBC are looking for songs to be submitted. Sandie Shaw is nominated as the performer. Come up with a song for Sandie.' We were just hungry to get some songs recorded. I remember sitting down and I remember saying this to Bill Martin. I know everybody is listening to all of Sandie Shaw's hits and trying to write a song for Sandie Shaw.

The trick here is, not to take your eyes off the main event. The main event here is the Eurovision Song Contest. We should be writing a song, not for Sandie Shaw (who happens to be the singer), but we should be writing for the Eurovision, so we have got to do our homework and listen to all the past hits of Eurovision and see what ticks the boxes in Europe and rings a bell for those people, and that was our approach, so 'Puppet on a String' was unlike any of her hits. I thought the big hurdle was to get over that first qualification. If we can actually win this British heat and get as far as Europe, I had a good feeling that the song can connect with a European audience. The tougher one was to persuade the British fans. Not only did it win, but it romped home. We outvoted the song that came second by about 5:1 or something.

It's a misconception that Phil and Bill (Coulter/Martin) shared the songwriting. Bill wasn't a musician but a great ideas man, and the best salesman Phil ever encountered. Nobody intimidated him and he was a natural promotions man, so while Phil did the bulk of the creative work, Bill did the bulk of the selling. There wasn't a door he wouldn't go through. He was one of those very in-your-face Glaswegians, and it was a chemistry that worked for many years. So, it was on to Vienna for the final, for Phil Coulter and Sean Dunphy. Dickie Rock recalls where he was that night:

Sean was a great pal of mine. While I knew his song was nice, I didn't expect it to do well at all, as it was very parochial. 'They envy me, those hills of Clare.' People wouldn't know when foreign countries were singing about a part of their country; I wouldn't know what it was about. I didn't expect him to do well, but it was a lovely song. That night when Sean Dumphy was singing in the Eurovision, I was working in Belfast. We had come fourth the previous year, and I remember asking Sammy Smith, the manager of Romano's, the ballroom in Belfast, to let me know where Sean came. It's human nature that I hoped he did well. But then Sammy looked over the balcony and I remember looking back at him, and he put the two fingers up and I thought, feck that.

Vienna 1967 was when Ireland's dominant songwriting grip on Eurovision began. The late Wesley Burrowes, and Michael Coffee, finished second with their composition 'If I Could Choose', and Phil Coulter took home the big prize, making it an Irish one-two. Phil remembers the aftermath of his success:

It was a runaway winner, and the excitement of that night was just uncanny. I remember running on stage just after it was announced. Remember, this was our first attempt, I was twenty-five years of age and this was our first outing into the big league. I rember hanging out with the Irish delegation: Sean Dunphy had sung for Ireland, and the late journalist Michael Hand. The BBC delegation was in another part of the hotel, but at that stage I didn't care, I just couldn't believe we'd pulled it off. There was an unreal sense of: Jesus Christ, we actually pulled it off.

I've often thought subsequently how I would have loved to have been in Derry. They told me afterwards, as there was a Derry boy involved, when the result was announced people came running out of their houses into the streets. There were big cheers and street parties going on. I'd love to have been around to see that, that kind of local-hero thing. The real moment I savoured, apart from the winning, was that we were the first ever songwriters to win it for the UK, so our place in history is now secured. We didn't come home on the Sunday, because we were hung over and couldn't make the flight. We thought to ourselves: we've won the Eurovision, cancel it, we'll get a flight on Monday. So Bill and I stayed in Vienna just trying to come to terms with the whole thing, and working our way through our hangover. The following day, coming back from

Heathrow Airport in a taxi, we pulled up at traffic lights and a truck pulled up alongside us and the truck driver was whistling 'Puppet on a String'. I'd never had that experience before. When I was learning my craft as a songwriter, publisher Jimmy Phillips would say: 'We know you've studied music at university for five years. You don't have to prove it every time you sit down to write a song. You want to think about the man driving the truck.' He's the guy you want to be thinking about when you're writing your song. So, I was in a taxi and the man driving the truck is whistling my song. That was the professional moment when I thought: I get it.

A few weeks later, back home in Derry, the city council gave me a civic reception, which consisted of a glass of dry sherry down at the mayor's parlour in the Guild Hall. They sent the mayor's car, an old Austin Princess, up to our terraced house to pick up my mother, father and me to go to the Guild Hall. Having studied music for all of those years in university, my mother's dearest wish was that I would go back and teach in St Columb's College in Derry, and get a proper job with a pension. They weren't really convinced that I'd made the right move to go to London and make a living out of what she'd call 'that jazz music'. She thought I was making a living by stealing hubcaps off cars, I think. All the neighbours were going 'That's the mayor's car.' That was a very fulfilling moment for my mother. That's one of my favourite recollections from the Eurovision.

In 1968 Tom McGrath had a lot more songs to choose from, so the National Final had two semi-finals. Roly Daniels, Dawn Knight, Leslie Cooke and Tommy Drennan were just some of those competing, and, making her debut, was Alma Carroll. Her first memories of the Eurovision were watching Gigliola Cinquetti win for Italy with '*Non Ho L'eta*' in 1964. Alma started her singing career as a soloist in the Young Dublin Singers Choir in St Louis School in Rathmines, before going into Jury's Irish Cabaret in Dame Street. She recalls:

That first year I was working with Jack Cruise in the Olympia Theatre. I was about sixteen, RTÉ came in, and it was Tom

McGrath. After the year Sean Dunphy came second, they came to different singers and said they wanted them to sing different songs. They asked me to sing *'Non Ho L'eta'*, and that led on to me being given 'Give Me All Your Love' and sadly, I didn't win.There were two semi-finals in 1968. The first year I sang it, they had a studio, and one of the people on the panel was the late P. V. Doyle. Gloria Hunniford definitely took part, and Pat McGeeghan was in that year as well, and he just had a beautiful voice.

'Puppet on a String' had gone global by now, with several different versions having been recorded, including one by a French Orchestra called Paul Mauriat. (His song 'Love is Blue' came fourth in 1967.) The album was called *Paul Mauriat Plays Puppet on a String and Other Blooming Hits'*, and as the months went by Phil was spending his time checking the trade press just to see where his song was a chart-topper (including Ireland and the UK). He was playing the part of a songwriter, without writing the songs. He continues:

> Our publisher called us in and said: 'Congrats guys, "Puppet on a String" is a fantastic song, but let me tell you something, one swallow never made a summer, and one song never made a songwriter. The business is now beginning to think of you guys as a flash in the pan.' I can remember to this day how that stung. I can remember him saying it. I can remember the room and I can remember that it just cut like a knife. 'Flash in the pan?' with some justification, because we haven't written anything, so we came out of that duly chastened by our publisher Jimmy Phillips, and I said. 'You know what, the only way to prove we're not a flash in the pan is to win the Eurovision all over again. Let's go and win it again.'

How crazy a thought was that for Phil and Bill? It was possibly the arrogance of youth also. Cliff Richard was the nominated artist for 1968 (after Cilla Black had turned it down), and in their naivety, Phil and Bill thought that the BBC would give them a free pass into the final, as they had won it the previous year. But they had to join the queue like everyone else, and all the songs were submitted anonymously. They decided with their Eurovision experience that it was either going to be a novelty song or a big powerful ballad. They reckoned nobody did the big powerful ballads better than the Italians, the French and the Spanish. Phil continues:

> 'Puppet on a String' worked because it had that fairground thing going on. We needed to come up with something, with a hook. I don't know if I've ever told this story before, but we started writing for the Eurovision when Jimmy Phillips said, 'I'm glad to see you're taking my advice', I came up with a song that had all the ingredients and was called 'My Magic Music Box'. I wrote a kind of a music-box theme going through it. Jimmy asked: 'Where are you doing the demos this time, boys?' We'd made the demo of 'Puppet on a String' for about thirty quid. Jimmy said: 'No, do a proper demo for "My Magic Music Box",' and then he said 'What else have you got?' and we said 'Nothing except "My Magic Music Box".' He said 'Well, it's not a bad song, but if we're gonna spend good money on the demo, we need another. So we left his office and went over to another office where there was a piano. I sat down at five o'clock in the afternoon and before going home at six I'd basically banged out what became the basis for 'Congratulations', but the real trick was, it wasn't a bad tune but it needed something, it needed a good hook to go all the way.

While Bill Martin has rewritten history a few times over the years, by stating in interviews that it could have been 'do you re-mem-ber' or 'I can't for-get you' or 'I al-ways love you', that was never the case. It could have been any of those and the song would have disappeared without a trace, but Bill was right that getting the song title was the key. Phil explains:

> I remember sitting at home and I had this rhyming dictionary. I was wondering: 'Is there a word with five syllables?' Seriously, and then I came across 'congratulations', and I thought there has to be a song called 'Congratulations', it's like 'Happy Birthday', but I can't think of one, so that's not

a bad idea. So once I got 'Con-grat-u-la-tions', the song kind of wrote itself: 'Congratulations, celebrations, jubilations'. That kind of informed what the arrangement was gonna be. You've got to remember that the metre starts running from the first second. You can't have, like, a four-bar intro with nothing going on. It has to grab you, it has to set the scene, it has to inform you of what's coming up, just like 'Puppet on a String'. With 'Congratulations', with the big brass dan-da-da-da-dan, dan-da-da-da-dan . . . boom boom boom boom, you're in already. Whatever's coming next, you're hooked. So that became 'Congratulations'. I thought, if we can only get through the British heats, and we walked it again. We were at the Royal Albert Hall with Cliff Richard, and we went in as favourites.

On the night of the final, the *London Evening Standard* had a banner headline across its front page. 'Can the Irishman and the Scotsman pull it off again?' That's how big the event was for the late Pat McGuigan (known then as Pat McGeegan), who was representing Ireland in London for the first Eurovision to be broadcast in colour. His son Barry would become a household name in 1985 when he became a world boxing champion, but even Pat found himself on the ropes that night, along with Phil, both suffering knockout punches from an unlikely Spanish winning song entitled 'La La La' in what was surely the biggest miscarriage of justice ever in the Eurovision. Phil recalls:

> I remember with a couple of countries to vote, we were well ahead in the Royal Albert Hall, and one of the BBC floor managers came up and called us out of our seats to be backstage, ready to go on and accept our reward. Bill Martin didn't want to leave; he said that's bad luck and didn't want to go. Anyway, we went, and we're standing at the side of the stage, and then to our great dismay, Germany gave six points to Spain and we're knocked back, and Spain wins by one point. They have to run down and get the Spanish writers on stage, and we're just numb.

The Massiel song would disappear without trace, possibly because its melody may have sounded similar to 'With a Little Help from My Friends', or because it was shite … Definitely the latter. Years later a Spanish journalist would make a revealing documentary, in which he interviewed television executives of the time and came up with an exposé detailing a directive from Franco and the powers-that-be. At that stage Spain was looking for acceptance, and Franco apparently felt that the Eurovision Song Contest would be a way of projecting Spain as a current, on-the-ball, glamorous country. So it was alleged that delegates from Spanish TV were sent into other television stations throughout Europe, at a time when juries judged the contest, and the said juries were appointed by the television companies, so while we may never prove it happened, it was certainly doable. Phil continues:

If I'd heard that story of that theory in the year or so after, when it was still hurting, I'd have been irate. I would have thought I'd been cheated out of my place in the history books. With the passage of time I can look back and say (a) I've probably mellowed a bit, and (b) 'Congratulations' has proven it was the winner. 'Congratulations' has fed, clothed and educated several of my children so I've no complaints about that, and people looking back on that still think 'Congratulations' won the Eurovision Song Contest, so history has a way of righting those wrongs. It certainly was a wrong, there's no doubt about it. I would say 'La La La' died within six months, whereas 'Congratulations' to this day is still a big performer. When I look at my performance royalties, 'Congratulations' is always there. Just recently, with the new royal baby, television stations all around the world were camped outside Buckingham Palace, and what did the band play? 'Congratulations'. So it has become part of the fabric of the musical landscape.

The acid-test of any song is its longevity. If a song has got legs, if a song has substance, the simple test is longevity. If it's been around for twenty or thirty years it's got legs, and it's got legs for some good reason. With Cliff and the different versions, it would have sold four to five million records, but more importantly it's still alive and it's still getting performed. There's not a brass band, there's not a military band, there's not a pop orchestra in the world that doesn't play it. There's hardly a radio station in Europe that, in a programme that is dedicated to birthdays, anniversaries or engagements, doesn't either play 'Congratulations' every week or 'Congratulations' as the signature tune. It's as alive today as it ever was.

To this day, on the wall in Phil's office is a disc presented to him by the record company EMI in 1981, with the inscription: 'Thank You Phil Coulter for writing the British Anthem of Celebration 'Congratulations.'

As the sixties drew to a close, the NSC was still attracting big names and Tom McGrath was way ahead of his time in his approach and his production of the event. When we think of the reality entertainment shows today, it's clear to see that Tom was ahead of the curve. Having chosen eight songs for the NSC Final, Tom brought back our previous four Eurovision entrants: Butch, Dickie, Sean and Pat, and paired each of them up with a lesser-known singer as part of the show. One such entrant was Muriel Day:

I was with the Dave Glover Showband, which had recently split up. So, Dave and I were doing cabaret till we regrouped as a band. We were down playing a gig in Cork, in what used to be the Arcadia. It was a Monday night and it was actually pouring down out of the heavens. Butch Moore walked in with his wife, well, the woman who later became his wife and he was going to New York but they had cancelled the flight because of the weather conditions. We were like ships in the night, all of us in the showbands. We passed one another on the road but didn't get the much of a chance to talk or hear each other a lot.

After the show Butch said to me: 'I've never really heard you sing. How come you never did the Eurovision? If I can get you an audition up in Dublin this week for the National Song Contest, will you go?' Of course I said yes, and he phoned someone, and on the Tuesday they called me and said could I come up on the Wednesday and audition for them. I went up to Dublin on the Wednesday and the late Mr Noel Kelehan was on the piano, there was no mi-crophone, and about five or six people at the table. I sang two songs for them and I came out and said to Dave Glover: 'Well, that's that.' On Friday they phoned me and said they had a song for me, so that's how I got into the National.

Along with Muriel, the remaining contestants were Dana, Eleanor Nodwell and Fiorenza Viana-Nolan. Dana remembers her first NSC:

> We were doing an opening medley of Eurovision-winning songs and I had to sing *'Poupee De Cire'*. We were lined up like a firing squad and the camera was panning along from one to the other. I thought I was going to die of nerves. I was thinking about running out because I felt I wasn't able for it. I remember being beside Butch Moore and he had a nervous habit when he was singing, he would rub the side of his leg, and it caught my attention. Then, all of a sudden the camera was on me and if it hadn't been for Butch Moore rubbing the side of his thigh, I would have been out of the door and out of the competition. I didn't want to win. I wouldn't have been able to cope with Eurovision and I just couldn't control my nerves. I've no doubt people were praying I was getting votes and I was praying that they didn't vote. I was delighted for Muriel Day, she deserved to win it.

Both the songs that finished first and second in the NSC were written by Dublin man Michael Reade, but it was Muriel who would become Ireland's first female Eurovision representative. She remembers that night vividly:

> I was paired with Dickie Rock, and Dickie sang 'Now Do You Believe Me'. I sang 'Love Is Blue'. There was sixty points on the board and 'The Wages of Love' got thirty, and the rest of the songs just shared the other thirty. It was amazing for me because I came down to Dublin, and just brought an overnight bag and my dresses. I was thinking I'd be back up there the next day but ended up staying a week because I won it. I recorded 'The Wages of Love' in Dublin and Dave wasn't happy with the arrangement, he thought we could do it better, so we re-recorded it in London. It didn't work as well, if

I'm being very honest. In those days, with me being married to Dave, I didn't really make a lot of the decisions.

Muriel set off for Spain in late March with her backing singers, The Lindsays. RTÉ had sent a big entourage out with Muriel, including the three backing singers, Tom McGrath and Noel Kelehan. There was quite a lot of media attention with Lulu participating, given her recent marriage to Maurice Gibb. Muriel remembers Madrid:

> When we got to Madrid we had rehearsals. They're doing it slightly different now with semi-finals and eliminations and so on. That didn't happen back then. Everybody who had come over to Madrid got picked to perform. Eventually we made friends with many of them and used to go out. We'd go to the old part of Madrid and have dinner and just talk and have a laugh. It was exciting and we got a chance to go to the Real Madrid Football Stadium and see all the cups in their trophy room. It was better for David than it was for me, but it was interesting. Lulu would have been one of the favourites and she was great, no doubt about it, but that year the best song was from the French girl Frida Boccara. It was called *'Un Jour, Un Enfant'* ('One Day, A Child'). It was magnificent. That's why there were four winners. Salome, the Spanish singer, was great, with *'Viva Cantanto'*. It was difficult to make a decision.

Gay Byrne was part of the media entourage with Muriel that week in Spain; he was commentating for television on his first Eurovision. Gay remembers Madrid:

> The only outstanding memory I have of that week is that a gang of us, including Adrian Cronin and and most of the team, went to the restaurant where Ernest Hemingway regularly dined, or so we were told, and we had roast suckling pig, which was his favourite dish. It was down a side street and you went up several flights of stairs to a tiny room and there

was a spit with a suckling pig roasting. You were served and this was the great big thrill that you had roast suckling pig in this restaurant just as Ernest Hemingway had done.

The final Eurovision Song Contest of the sixties took place at Madrid's Teatro Real Opera House with Muriel singing fifth on the night and finishing joint seventh. Her dressmaker Alice Campbell made the dress. At first it looks green, but it's not. It's a green, white and gold dress. If you look carefully you'll see the yellow underneath the green, then the silver. Even today, her performance still looks confident and professional, but Muriel says otherwise:

> On the night I was terrified, but that's showbiz and the showband upbringing. You go out and you're terrified and you just open your mouth. My problem is, even now, I get very nervous, but the minute I get the first four lines out of me, then I'm OK. You ask any singer and I'm sure they'll say the same. You're terrified when you walk out, but the minute the music starts, the minute you sing the first couple of lines, that's it. It was nerve-racking knowing that it was on live television. You knew it was going to be watched by all of Europe but the Opera House in Madrid seated five thousand. It was packed and people were all dressed up in evening gowns and jewellery. You could see all the jewellery flashing. It was like a live show; forget about the viewers, you had five thousand people in there. We finished joint fourth. There were four songs tied for joint first but none of the twenty-eight judges would give in so they actually had four number ones. We were joint fourth. It annoyed me, simply because it's never happened again.

Lulu's manager Peter Warne co-wrote 'Boom Bang a Bang'. He would go on to write a couple of songs for Muriel, including 'Nine Times out of Ten'. It wouldn't be until 2015 that Muriel would release her debut album, but in 1969, her Eurovision song topped the Irish singles charts and gave Muriel something else to be proud of:

I was aware that I had gone to number one in the Irish charts at the time but what had made me laugh was that I had knocked Marvin Gaye off the charts. It was absolutely ridiculous. To say that you knocked Marvin Gaye off the charts is embarrassing. I've been back to Spain, but not to Madrid. One day I think I will go back and see what it is like nowadays. At Eurovision everything was so exciting. Winning would have been fantastic. Still, it was all good fun. I wouldn't trade it for the world.

CHAPTER TWO

ALL KINDS OF EVERYTHING

Most notable about the 1970 NSC was the increase in Irish-language submissions, with three songs making the final. Anna McGoldrick and Tony Kenny were back again, having both participated for the first time two years previously. Also making their debut this year was Maxi, Dick and Twink.

They had met in school when they were about ten or eleven, and became friends in the school choir. They worked in the Gaiety summer shows, and were discovered by Eamonn Andrews, who was looking for a trio to sing backing vocals on a showband disc. Maxi (Irene McCoubrey), Dick (Barbara Dixon) and Twink (Edele King) passed the auditions because their voices blended. Coming home from school about half past four, they'd go into the studio and record backing vocals on various showband songs, beginning around 1966. Maxi recalls her first NSC:

> We'd done television shows with Jim Doherty and Des Smyth for a season called 'Steady as You Go-Go' which was set on a ship. Then Jim and Des wrote the song 'Things You Hear About Me' and submitted it. We sang it at the 1970 National Song Contest. We obviously wanted to win, but were so busy touring the country anyway, and any appearance on television meant that you wouldn't see the floorboards for the next year. We would have liked to have won, when you go in and you are one of eight. We felt vindicated when Dana won because the best song was chosen, but we got the publicity out of it, we got the work out of it, and the exposure, so we were contented to get on television at that stage.

Maxi, Dick and Twink weren't the first act to sing 'Things You Hear About Me', as it had been recorded prior to the NSC, as Alma Carroll explains:

> Jim Doherty wrote a song for me called 'Things You Hear About Me' that was put into the Eurovision. Maxi, Dick and Twink were very popular at the time and were on television a lot. I don't know who it was but somebody gave Maxi, Dick and Twink the song. I had recorded it but I wasn't allowed release it, as it had gone into the NSC. I was very upset at that time.

The experience from the previous year would stand to Dana this time round. Her nerves on this occasion were not evident, and she grabbed the moment:

> Tom McGrath matched me to the song. He had a Midas touch, whether it was the shows he was doing or linking up songs to singers, he had a real gift. I didn't think of it as a winning song, though I thought it was a really nice song. It was quite like a folk song, I was a folk singer at this time, so it suited me very well. I honestly never dreamt it would win. Not because of the song, but because the thought of me winning was impossible.

Despite his track record Phil Coulter was surprisingly never approached by RTÉ to submit a song for Eurovision. It was only because he was over in Dublin on completely different business and invited out to RTÉ to watch the rehearsals, that he got involved with the Irish entry in the first place. Phil explains:

> John Murphy said 'I'm working on the National Song Contest out in RTÉ. Why don't you come out to that and then we'll go on the piss.' So I went out, and in the middle of rehearsals I see this wee girl from Derry, Rosemary Brown, singing this cute folksy song. The arrangement wasn't right but there was just something about the purity of it. I thought, *Now if this could get through to Europe and was done in the right order after some*

boom-bang-a-bangs and some big brassy stuff, it's a breath of fresh air, this could really collect, I thought, *because it's very different.* I chatted to the two lads who had written it, Derry Lindsey and Jackie Smith. In 1969 we weren't involved because we were getting established. I signed 'All Kinds of Everything' to our company, which gave me control over the song and the orchestration. I was able to give it a bit of Eurovision fairy dust. I changed the intro. I remember it went 'di-di-dit-dit-dit dit . . . brr brr'. Every percussion player has that sound in his bag of tricks. In those days it really was made with the jaw-bone of an ass [*oujida*], and you had to give it a kind of a karate chop. It went 'grrr'. I always thought it was a cute little sound. I've used it on a few arrangements, and when I heard 'All Kinds of Everything', I thought, *that's a place I could use that sound.* I remember at the rehearsals in Amsterdam the percussion player didn't have a jaw-bone of an ass. I remember calling Michael Hand, a journalist, who was flying out the next day to cover the competition. I got one delivered to him and he brought it out. When Dana performed she looked so pure and folksy. It was a great feeling knowing your instincts were right.

While Phil wasn't credited as the producer of the song, there was a different definition of the term back then. For all intents and purposes, he produced it, and it's his arrangement. It was on to the bright March lights of Amsterdam for Dana. She'd only ever been to England once before; these were exciting times for a teenager. She was unhappy with the dress that RTÉ wardrobe had designed. It had a high neck with a little white collar and was green and short-sleeved. Dana felt that it made her look like Shirley Temple; she wanted something that was more contemporary.

I'm not sure if the girl who designed that dress was from the west, but the embroidery on the dress was done in the west of Ireland. I loved the dress and loved the fact that it was a contemporary shape. I loved the fact that it was traditional *boinin* material, and I loved the adaptation of the Irish dancing embroidery because it was a contemporary twist on something traditional. Those styles have come

around again. Since 'Riverdance' there has been a real sense
of pride in what we wear. My mother and my grandmother
travelled with me and the Irish team, and we were mes-
merised by Amsterdam. It was freezing. Nobody bothered
us because Ireland had never won, so nobody expected us
to win. The only people who took photographs and did
interviews with me were the Irish journalists and one young
guy who couldn't be there on the night; he interviewed
everybody. I remember walking around, and of course you
were nearly afraid to go in anywhere, or buy anything. I
remember a great sense of relief when we turned the corner
and there was a Wimpy.

As was by now routine, the build-up to the big night consisted of rehearsals, sound-
checks and a run-through with the orchestra. Noel Kelehan wasn't there, so it was
the host conductor, the late Dolf Van Der Linden, who conducted Dana's performance. She was up against some big talent, including Germany's Katja Ebstein,
the then unknown Spaniard Julio Iglesias, and the favourite, Mary Hopkins, but
favourites were the furthest thing from Dana's mind on the night. She had a bigger
obstacle to overcome before she even sang a note:

I sat on a cylinder that was very difficult to sit on. You could-
n't get your foot up on it and that was a big worry, and if you
sat on it crooked you'd be frightened for your life. If you
were too far forward you could slide down the front, which
was a huge worry for me, getting down the slope. It was
sloped, and first of all I was afraid of slipping on the slope,
then I was afraid of not getting on the stool properly. You
forget about that once you're seated and you concentrate on
the song. I was OK. We were all seated in one room around
a table and television as the voting came in. There was a
lovely relaxed atmosphere. Everybody cheered when anyone
got a vote. They moved us from there out to the side of the
stage where there was another television, so we were all
grouped around the television. I wasn't interested in the voting. I was just concentrating on the people around me. I was
star-struck. Suddenly the late Jackie Smith ran out to congratulate me. I wasn't aware I'd won until the stage manager

grabbed my arm and pulled me to the stage. I was pulling against him, and Mary Hopkins was saying: 'You've won!' I was in shock for about six months afterwards.

John Kennedy O'Connor is the official Eurovision Song Contest biographer. Long before John became interested in the Eurovision, he knew Ireland was going to win in 1970:

> I remember my grandfather dying around April 1970, and my mother telling me that she had just heard the Irish Eurovision song and that they were going to win by a mile. You never heard somebody else's song before the big night in those days, but she was right, of course, and Dana ran away with the contest.

As Ireland's first-ever winner of the Eurovision, the homecoming was a memorable occasion for Dana. It is something that will live long in her memory:

> We landed in Dublin first; I'd won for Ireland. They had a new plane in Aer Lingus and they had put wording along the side of the plane that read 'Operation Dana'. We landed and they opened the door of the plane and I walked out. They estimated there to have been five thousand people in the old terminal building, and anytime I go through Dublin Airport it always crosses my mind. They were on the roof and on the balconies. It was just like the bow of a ship. Everybody was just screaming, shouting and cheering. I had never seen anything like it. We then flew up to Ballykelly, which is just outside of Derry. It was the first time that a Republic of Ireland aircraft had landed in British airspace in Northern Ireland; it was the first time that Aer Lingus had ever landed in Northern Ireland in their own plane. There were thousands there as well. It was a more intimate reception with family and friends. I went in a big black car and met the head of the council. People were lined all the way along, waving and cheering. By the time we got to the centre, we couldn't get into Guild Hall Square. The crowd surrounded the car; they lifted me out and carried me shoulder-to-shoulder into the Guild Hall. It was

amazing. I'll never forget it. We lived in the bogside flats at that time. I got gorgeous bouquets covered in cellophane, and I was greeted by the neighbours. There'd been a problem and the water had been turned off in the flats. So I put the flowers in the bath, but there was no water when I went to turn the tap on to feed the flowers. After discovering that they had turned off all the water, I went off to the pictures with my younger brother Gerald. When I came back, the water had come back on, because I hadn't turned the tap off completely at all. Our flat, the flat below and the flat below that were all flooded. My mother said when she stepped onto the carpet, the water was up to her ankles. I'm sure they'd have killed me were they not so delighted about the win.

Paul Lyttle of Chips remembers Dana's win:

I remember seeing Muriel Day and then Dana. Chips had just turned professional that year that Dana won. I remember our reaction as a band was that the Irish music business had changed forever. To an extent, it did. We had never won anything internationally before; it opened the door. People came to Ireland instead of Ireland trying to get out and go to other countries. It was a major step forward regardless of what you think of the songs. It's the business part that mattered.

Dana agrees with Paul:

When I won the Eurovision Decca didn't have the master; it was with Rex Records. The man that deserves an accolade is Michael Geoghegan. He was the head of Rex Records in Dublin. Phil Mitton was his secretary. Rex was just a big distributing company for Decca, as Decca was the big company and Rex Records was the Irish distributor. Michael had it in his head, though, that they had great talent here, and he wanted to make sure that they had a break. There was myself, Joe Cuddy, Sonny Knowles, Patricia Cahill and loads of others. Phil Mitton entered me in for the auditions for the contests, so when I was on holiday and they [Decca] didn't dream that I was going to win, they didn't even have a master. When I won there was absolute pandemonium. It was probably the first time in the history of Decca Records, one of the biggest companies in the world, that a distributing company outsold another company. They had to press on Rex Records. It was quite an incredible achievement for Michael Geoghegan and Rex Records.I performed on *Top of the Pops* when it went to the top ten, and I did it at least two or three more times when the song was number one. It knocked 'Bridge Over Troubled Water' off number one. We were all delighted at the time. There are people I really thank for that. Tom McGrath, Michael Geoghegan, and of course Phil Mitton. Certainly Tom and Michael were outstanding. The song-writers, [Jackie Smith and Derry Lindsay] they were two amateurs, like me. There is something about that song, everywhere you go in Europe, people just love it. It's wonderful hearing people's memories of that song.

On 3 April 1971, Ireland hosted the Eurovision Song Contest for the first time. Tom McGrath was the producer and director, and RTÉ chose the Gaiety Theatre on South King Street for the event. Hosting the event was an ideal opportunity to sell Ireland as a tourist attraction, and RTÉ capitalised on this with Stuart Hetherington's opening film featuring Grace O'Shaugnessy and Brian McGrath being collected from a house in Merrion Square and taken in a white, horse-drawn carriage through the capital, taking in the scenery. They went up through Stephen's Green and arrived at the Gaiety Theatre, where the crowd were shown arriving for that night's contest. RTÉ pulled out all the stops. It was one of their first events to be broadcast in colour. Ken Shannon was the head cameraman, and the sound desk was fitted with twenty-four channels. Bernadette Ní Ghallchóir introduced the contest wearing a full, flowing green dress, and the Shannon Castle Entertainers would provide the interval entertainment. Ian McGarry, who was part of the orchestra that night, remembers this momentous occasion:

> It was massive. Dana had won it previously and it was the first time we had staged it. My memories are very much of rehearsals. Drums are at the centre of everything that

happens on stage. As the drummer, you're the timer for everything that goes on, and the artists expect from you only the highest quality. The Gaiety was very confining, as the full orchestra was in the pit. They extended the pit a little bit but it was literally just under the stage. There was a big reception afterwards. I snuck in with some of the technical guys whohad been invited.

Also in attendance at the Gaiety that night, but in a working capacity, was Gay Byrne:

> People all over the country were stabbing each other in the back to get tickets to be at it, but there were only seats for six hundred people. We ended up doing the Eurovision Song Contest in the Gaiety Theatre. Adrian Cronin directed, and I was in my dickie bow and my lovely tuxedo. I was the scorekeeper, overseen by Clifford Brown the scrutineer. There wasn't a seat for me because the theatre was very crowded. The normal seating in the Gaiety would have been about eight hundred, but it was reduced to six hundred on account of the ceremony.

Portadown teenager Angela Farrell was Ireland's representative, with her song 'One Day Love' having seeing off Red Hurley and Danny Doyle, amongst others, in the National, but she sadly could not repeat that success in the Grand Prix and had the misfortune of being our first entrant not to finish in the top ten. The winner that night was Severine from Monaco with *'Un Banc, Un Arbre, Une Rue'*. Dana was there to present the winner with flowers, and she recalls how proud she was:

> I presented the winner with the prize, which was great. I had a song called 'Who Put the Lights Out', which was in the charts all over Europe. It saved me, and in a way it saved Ireland. If a winner came out of Ireland capable of remaining in the pop scene, then they couldn't call Ireland a one-hit wonder. It may have been then that Ireland got colour

TV. They had an oral agreement with BBC for the hiring of colour cameras. I was so proud that night, and I thought Ireland put on an amazing production.

Bill Whelan, a Limerick man, who would go on to be synonymous with the Eurovision in the eighties and nineties, was a young musician learning his trade in the early seventies and was involved with several of the NSCs.

> I went off to work with RTÉ as a young arranger, and on a number of occasions I played the piano on the selection panel. People used to send in sheet music but mostly cassettes or reel-to-reel tapes. I became aware of how the voting worked but there was a thing that we had to have an Irish song (if memory serves me correctly) in the last eight, or whatever it came down to. I remember people used to send in songs in Irish because they had a better chance of getting through, and I often remember there was a particular year that I was on the panel and a guy sent in a song. There was a service, in those days, to have demos. You sent your song off to a company who made a demo of your song with professional music. He had sent his song to England, though, and had a demo made in Irish, so this English singer had to deal with the Irish, and it came back as a garbled load of nonsense.

There were a great many Irish songs in the 1978 NSC. Over half of the final selection were sung in Gaelic. Joe Cuddy was there with *'Mo Dhuachas Dún Na Ngall'* ('My Lovely Donegal'), Lola sang *'Óro Áine'* ('Precious Anne'), The Farrells sang *'Bualadh Bos'* ('Clap Your Hands'), and Paddy Murphy and Maire O'Shea duetted on *'Tar Liom'* ('Come With Me'), but it was Sandie Jones, singing *'Ceol An Ghrá'* (Music of Love) that beat off Des Smyth and made history as the first Gaelic song to represent Ireland at the Eurovision. Written by Joe Burkett and Liam MacUistin, it would fail to impress the judges in Edinburgh, and Sandie finished a disappointing fifteenth, but it didn't deter songwriters from continuing to submit songs in Irish. A year later, half of the final entries were once more in Gaelic. Barbara Dixon (Dick, of Maxi, Dick and Twink) was back again, Clannad, who would go on to have success in the eighties, were in the final for the first time, and Danny Doyle was back again to improve on his fourth-place finish two years earlier. Maxi was now a member of Danny's band, but she went solo for the NSC that year, when she was offered the song 'Do I Dream', written by Jack Brierley (who was a resident musician at the Stardust in Cork), and George Crosbie (who was one of the owners of the *Cork Examiner*). Maxi recalls:

> I was thrilled when I was approached to do the song, as I have deep respect for Jack and George, and winning the National Song Contest was such an honour. I loved the song and I loved the idea of travelling, having a taste for it, as I'd lived in Canada and the States. I had listened to Radio Luxembourg under the duvet. I really wanted to go to Luxembourg (a) to represent my country, and (b) to visit Radio Luxembourg. I met Pete Murray and Kid Jensen and Tony Blackburn - all the greats. I did an interview with Pete for the BBC. When we were finished he said: 'Your voice is beautiful on the radio. Have you ever thought of doing radio broadcasts? Just in case you get a chance in your career when you're not singing, think of doing a radio course. His words came back to me when I was in Sheeba. We had had a bad car accident in 1981, and I was the most badly injured. The girls had gone home, and I lay back listening to the radio. I thought: My God Almighty, I would love to do that. So I sent off audition tapes, even though nobody had asked me to audition, and got the job. Kevin Hough was my producer, and it became my career.

If Radio Luxembourg was part of the attraction for Maxi, there was more to come. It was a case of right place, right time. Her adventure was about to get even more exciting:

> It was at the Holiday Inn in Luxembourg. They had organised lifts to the event for the different countries, depending on your rehearsal time, and I was sitting outside waiting for my bus to come. The Holiday Inn bus pulled up, and the side door opened, and Cliff Richard asked me:

'Would you like a lift?' and I said: 'Oh yes.' I thought, I'm going to upset the whole schedule now, because the Irish bus will pull up and will be looking for me, but then I thought, this is an offer I can't refuse. So I sat beside Cliff and talked away. Then he said: 'Would you like to come for a photo-shoot?' I still have that photo. I just adored Cliff Richard. He was the cherry on the cake when I won the National Song Contest, and he was representing the UK. The support from one professional artist to another was amazing. He could have easily just gone by and said: 'Well, her bus is coming along behind mine.' I believe in positivity and putting things out there and wishing for them. Cliff Richard had been on my wall as a child, the same with McCartney. It happened, and I believed it would happen, because when I heard Cliff was representing the UK, the journalist was saying: 'Well, you won't meet him because he'll be protected', but I was saying 'I know I will.' So, sitting out that day waiting for the lift, I thought the Irish van would come along with Holiday Inn written on it, and it was Cliff, and I said: 'Yeah.' Nobody can take that away.

The media were reporting back to Ireland during the rehearsals that all was not well in the Irish camp and that Maxi had a problem with the song. RTÉ put Tina Reynolds on standby. Maxi sets the record straight:

I never refused to sing 'Do I Dream'. There was a taste thing, a beat rhythm, but don't forget that there are lots of things done for publicity. I was just doing my gig and rang home, and somebody said that I was all over the papers, and I replied, 'Not for the first time.' The late Tom McGrath will tell you that from the grave. Tina was on standby. She and I were the best of buddies, and she got next year's. The press never got that we're all pals, and would meet in the chipper on the way home from the gig and say 'Howya'. A friend of mine, a British journalist, said, 'The thing about the Eurovision is that when you go to it, there's five days before anything happens. As a journalist, you've got to make stuff happen to keep it in the papers. Cliff came up to me afterwards – you know when they go out and show your face for the votes – and he said to me, 'I'm not going out [he was supposed to sit beside me], so there will be an empty chair. I'm just not going to let them see my face.' I said thanks for telling me, but I'm not going to do that. Winning got you a lot of exposure. The actual show meant that you had tonnes of record sales. It was very lucky being in Luxembourg. There was a lot of publicity through Radio Luxembourg, which did me a power of good. Winning was fantastic, but not getting first didn't mean that you didn't get the premiere attention. Artists go in thinking about what they'll get from this exposure, and meeting the DJs. Winning is, of course, an honour, and something very special, but if you don't win, does it mean you lose?

Tina Reynolds was rewarded for her loyalty. To ensure that Tina would be Ireland's representative in Brighton, Tom McGrath invited her to sing all eight songs in the NSC final. Paul Lyttle, songwriter and guitarist with Chips, was all in favour of Tina performing all the songs:

> I thought it was a great idea because the most popular song at the time won. There were, in fairness, better songs, but it's the public's choice. I only wrote 'Cross Your Heart', and Adrian Mullen, who was the keyboard player in Chips, wrote 'My World', so we had two representations in there. She [Tina Reynolds] had to sing all eight songs in the National Song Contest. She had to use 'idiot boards', where the lyrics were placed around the stage, so that when she wasn't looking at the camera she could glance down and make sure she was right. She more or less had it nailed, but she had a terrible time before that. I was still so pleased that she got to do that. She had had a serious accident a year earlier. I think she was involved in another accident just afterwards and broke her leg again. She had a really rough time. The night of the National Song Contest final was fine for me until the winner was announced, and then the rest is a blur. It was a social highlight in the television calendar, and naturally a way for the whole island to root for Ireland, which was a great thing. It was the biggest live TV concert for many years. I think every middle-of-the-road musician aspired to it, because there was no way

out for middle-of-the-road musicians back then, unless you moved country or got a record deal. There was simply nowhere to go, and the Eurovision was a way of getting out and spreading your wings. It was fantastic, because all of Europe watched it and all of Europe was mad about it. All you had to do was appear on it and your profile went up fifty percent, it was remarkable. It was like an early reality show – it was unbelievable. That week of going to the Eurovision is well documented as being the best week of most musicians' lives. As well as getting to represent Ireland, it is so worthwhile on every level, both for business and making friends.

With the Eurovision in Brighton and the BBC in control, the presenter was Katie Boyle. According to Paul:

I didn't get my week at the Eurovision. Chips were working the UK and we were humping up and down it, and I got Friday night and Saturday in Brighton, so I saw the dress rehearsal and the show, and that was it. Olivia Newton-John was the favourite. When I arrived on Friday, everyone was talking about her. But they hadn't seen Abba, fully dressed for the dress rehearsal. I'll never forget sitting in the Dome in Brighton as part of the Irish delegation, watching all the songs. Olivia came on and I thought she was fantastic and beautiful, and the song really helped. Then there was this brilliant Dutch duo called Mouth and MacNeal, who were very big in their home country and also very big when the Eurovision came on. Then Tina came on and did her thing. I was very happy and very proud. It sounded fantastic. Then bloody Abba came on and we all just put our heads in our hands. Out they came in those ridiculous costumes, and it just worked. It was so fresh, so new and so incredible. It was the winner. I sat there for the interval act. I had to sit through Uncle Bulgaria. The Wombles were huge then, and Mike Batt was a genius. The music was incredible, it was orchestral pop. I wouldn't agree that 'Waterloo' was the best Eurovision Song ever, but it started a fantastic career. It was a great Eurovision year, I thought. Then again, I was glad that the year I got to do it, the BBC were running it, because the BBC orchestra were incredible. Their sound and staging is legendary. I was very fortunate to be involved in that one.

Brothers Tommy and Jimmy Swarbrigg had been in the music business for years. They grew up in Cootehill, County Cavan, and were aware of the Eurovision long before Ireland took part in 1965. UK acts like Ronnie Carroll and husband-and-wife duo Teddy Johnson and Pearl Carr were some of their earliest memories, and as Tommy explains, they always wanted to take part in it:

> I'd a great interest from the word 'go', and it was an ambition back then to take part in it one day. Whatever about the Eurovision, even when it began, the National Song Contest was ginormous. The country came to a standstill. It was as big as the Eurovision itself. There was voting all over the country, and I was just as addicted as everybody else. I made it my business to watch it wherever we were playing. The pinnacle of your songwriting, I thought, would be to get into the National Song Contest and then to win it. The exposure was pivotal, but I'd like to point out that we did have a lot of hit records before the Eurovision Song Contests. We had built a good career beforehand, but the Eurovision made us household names. No matter who you were, you became a household name by winning the National Song Contest and representing your country, because literally everyone watched it. You had the BBC if you were up around the border, but if you were down the country you only had your RTÉ, so it was huge. It also led to us getting international contracts, both publishing and recording, so there were a lot of positives.

Just like Tina a year earlier, the format remained in place in 1975 of one act singing all eight songs in the National Final, and The Swarbriggs were only too delighted to be involved. Tommy elaborates:

Tom McGrath, the RTÉ producer of the contest, actually offered us all of the songs to sing. He just came up to the National Ballroom one night and said, 'I want to talk to you afterwards, boys'. It was a pleasure, because everyone knew Tom in the business. He did all the light-entertainment stuff in RTÉ. He said 'I'd like you to sing all the songs in the National Song Contest.' It was a no-brainer. We couldn't lose – one way or another, we were going to be singing in it. We were allowed to submit one song as part of the deal. Ours was one of the eight chosen. We wrote 'That's What Friends Are For'. We were absolutely over the moon when it won out in the studios in RTÉ, and there was an enormous audience for the National Song Contest. It was as big as the Eurovision, and I'm not exaggerating. The country came to a standstill. Like the Eurovision, you had juries ringing in from about twelve different areas in the country: the Cork fury, the Galway jury, the Dublin jury, the Belfast jury, you name it.

Tommy and Jimmy wouldn't be the only Irish performers in Stockholm. Geraldine Brannigan from north Dublin had sung in the 1973 NSC final as part of the Brannigan sisters, when they finished fourth with '*Fadó Fadó*' ('Long Long Ago'). Now she would get the chance to perform solo.

Phil Coulter stepped away from the Eurovision after 1970. At that time, Luxembourg would have had the best track record in Eurovision. Given the size of the country, they would cherry-pick performers from their neighbours, like France or Germany. Though a small country, Luxembourg had a disproportionate influence in Europe through Radio Luxembourg and Radio Luxembourg Television, which were broadcast across Europe. Phil Coulter explains:

I was approached by Luxembourg through Radio Luxembourg UK. Their approach indicated that they took the Eurovision entries very seriously and had been doing their homework. 'There's nobody with a better track record right now than you,' they said, 'so we're giving you the commission. There's no competition, we're asking you to write the song and find the singer to represent Luxembourg. The only caveat is, it has to be sung in French.' I speak French, so that's not a problem.

Phil auditioned singers in the UK, but nothing really excited him, so while he was back in Dublin, he was in Jury's Hotel, about to go out for dinner. He had just had a shower and was lying on his bed watching television when he saw something that would change his life. Phil takes up the story:

> On comes an ad for Guinness, and it's set in a club. There's a band on stage and a girl with long hair singing. It's a look that would work in Eurovision: that long hair, those great cheekbones. I made a few enquiries to find out who was the agency, and who it was, and they said it's a singer called Geraldine Brannigan. To cut a long story short, I got the number and made an appointment, and was at Geraldine's front door at 10 AM ringing the doorbell, and Geraldine answered. Well, bingo! Six kids later, here we are. So we got Geraldine over to audition in the UK, and ticked all the boxes. Everyone asked where we'd found her, and said she was brilliant. I contacted an old songwriting pal of mine called Pierre Cour (of 'Love is Blue' fame) to do the lyrics. He was a well-established lyricist, very French, and smoked Gauloise cigarettes. He terrified the life out of Geraldine, so she was bricking it every time she had to meet him. I remember we were leading at the halfway mark, and that there was great excitement in the green room. It was too early to count your chickens, and we finished a credible fifth. It was a big ask, getting a girl from Clontarf to sing in French and represent another country, but she did great. That's why the Eurovision has a special place in this house.

The Swarbriggs also remember Stockholm. As Tommy recalls, there was one notable absence:

> We were there for a week, which was interesting. There were big parties and loads of receptions to go to. We had a great time. It was an amazing experience. We met everybody, including The Shadows. Everybody that was in it knew it was a lottery. Nobody could say who was going to win it, and it

was actually very close that year. I had a bad chest infection and I could barely sing. Amazingly, Abba were not invited to the contest. We met Benny and Bjorn in a radio station studio in Stockholm. I asked them if they were coming to the show and they said that they hadn't been invited. We were gobsmacked. Pete Murray from the BBC was doing the interviews, and they went in first. They were lovely guys. We sat in the waiting room, and then we went in and did our stint, and never saw them again. Even Pete Murray was stunned, as they were in no way involved in it. I do remember that it was a very open contest. Teach-In were surprise winners. I certainly didn't expect them to win: the song was a quiet little ditty, whereas we had the message song. In hindsight, ours was just too wordy, though it was hugely popular in Ireland.

CHAPTER THREE

BRENDAN'S VOYAGE

Brendan Graham was into music from an early age. Born in Tipperary, he got his first guitar when he was sixteen and learnt to play songs like 'Apache'. Being a member of the Kiltormer Ceili Band, he also played a few gigs around Ballinasloe. He moved to London in the mid-sixties, and played bass with a band called The Moonshiners. He took part in a talent competition there, and recalls doing a terrible version of 'Please Please Me', and how they got nowhere despite thinking they were the bee's knees. It was in London where the songwriting started. Brendan explains:

> I remember we used to go to this Chinese restaurant. I didn't have much money at the time, and sent money home. When I ran out of money I'd go down there and get a bowl of the dumpling soup because there was eating and drinking in it. The place had red serviettes, and one evening I was thinking about 'Eleanor Rigby', which was out about that time, a song I loved. I loved the imagery in it ('picks up the rice in a church where a wedding has been . . . '), and I thought about Father McKenzie. He was kind of a peripheral character in the song. I started writing this song called 'Father Dickens'. Later, when we were living in Mullingar, I had become friends with the Drifters and Joe Dolan. I became friends with Tommy Swarbrigg, and I was fascinated that they were writing songs, as I didn't know anybody else at the time doing that. I remember giving him the lyrics to look at. Then we went to Australia. We moved from Perth to

Melbourne, and that Christmas a battered package arrived. When I opened it up it was Johnny McEvoy's second album, *With an Eye To Your Ear*. Johnny was in this kind of velvet coat on the cover, looking at the album, and there amongst 'Here There And Everywhere', '59th St Bridge Song' and 'So Long Marianne' was 'Father Dickens'. It was a gorgeous arrangement, a Beatles-esque arrangement, with strings and everything. Tommy and his brother Jimmy had put music to it, and had added a bit of a bridge. I was totally chuffed, and then I was gutted. My name wasn't anywhere to be seen. It was a genuine error, but the sheer joy was in just seeing the song. Someone sent me a review that Shay Healy had in *Spotlight* magazine. He picked out the three best songs on the album: 'Here, There and Everywhere', 'So Long Marianne' and 'Father Dickens.' That gave me the incentive to write. I got a royalty cheque for something like one pound thirteen shillings and eleven pence. I never cashed the cheque, for two reasons. First, I thought, I might never get another cheque. The other reason was that I thought, if I can't do better than this, I should give up.

It was on his return to Ireland that Brendan became more aware of the Eurovision Song Contest. He did not have a television while living in Ballinasloe, but while walking down the street one evening he saw a crowd around the window of an electrical shop. The Eurovision was on. Now he wanted to be a part of it. Brendan explains:

Red Hurley had burst onto the scene. I remember turning on the radio one day and hearing this fantastic voice. I thought to myself that if I ever got the right type of song, he's the singer I would want for it. That was how it all started. I worked in a company called Trades of Ireland at the time, and I was getting a lift home with a guy who worked with me, who lived in Windy Arbour in Dublin. As we were driving in, I saw this young man out shining this nice, shiny car. The guy who was giving me the lift said 'That's Red Hurley, he lives in there'. So one evening I went up to Red's door (as I'm sure many others have), and I said, 'I'm writing songs, and I have a song here that you might like.' I had a song called 'Jacqueline', I think, that I gave to him. He liked it, and then he asked whether I had anything else. I was working on 'When' at the time, and played him a bit of that. He said, 'That's the one', so I finished it off, and Red did the demo of it. I think Liam [Hurley] played on it as well. All of a sudden the song began to be something, and the next thing I knew I got a telegram from RTÉ asking me to contact them. I didn't actually twig it that I had qualified. I thought they wanted to ask me something about the song, and then they told me that the song had gone through. It had no chorus, so we had to re-work it. Roberto Danova was producing Joe Dolan at the time, and I remember, on one occasion, how he kept me up all night in the Tara Towers Hotel in Dublin. I had a job at the time. I remember finishing work and Roberto kept saying, 'Why don't you do this' and 'Do that', and I went straight home, had a shower and went straight into work.

The competition in the 1976 NSC was tough. The Swarbriggs were back again with 'The Way Of Love', Cathal Dunne had a beautiful song called 'Danny', and Chips made their debut appearance. Linda Martin remembers her first contest:

I'll tell you what happened in those days. A man who I absolutely love called Tom McGrath, who has now sadly passed away, was in total control of the Eurovision participants and of the National Song Contest. He took great pride in it. I went to the Montrose Hotel, up beside RTÉ, and I sang a couple of songs for him while he sat behind a table with a few other people. You were put on a list until Tom found a song that would suit you, or doubled you up with somebody else or put you in a group. That was the process. I was put on the list, and we just waited for the opportunity, and the opportunity obviously came through, with Dana's brother. We all knew Dana's family and are still very close to them: lovely people. Her brother came up with 'We Can Fly', and they approached Louis and asked whether Chips would be interested in singing the song. Louis said 'Yes!' We said 'Yes!' And away we went. That was our first incursion into the NSC. We were actually signed to an

English record company at that point, Decca Records. They were in Ireland with us during the whole process. Oh God, how I cried when we lost. You've got to remember, we were still in our teens. It was our first time in the content, and our first time losing. I never cried after that, but that was the first time. If we had secured the win, Decca were poised to move into Europe with us, so it was a big deal. There was a lot depending on that win.

Louis Walsh, a fan of the Eurovision, grew up in Mayo watching Sandie Shaw on a big black-and-white TV in boarding school. During the seventies and eighties he would become synonymous with Irish Eurovision acts. He recalls:

My first involvement in the National Song Contest was with Chips. It was the biggest thing at the time, because you'd have a massive record in Ireland and possibly in Europe. I thought Chips were perfect, the perfect act. They just never seemed to get the right song, while we kept trying and trying.

Brendan Graham, however, has fonder memories:

Winning it was great, and fair play to Red for inviting me into his house that day, because I'm sure he gets loads of songs. I didn't know that at the time, and I think Liam [Hurley] and Johnny Tate orchestrated it. All of a sudden, it sounded great, but Red made a lot more out of the song than what was in the song. There was no chorus and no hook. He really made it sound like something.

The Eurovision was back in the Netherlands for the first time since Dana's victory, but this time they didn't opt for Amsterdam. Brendan Graham brought his parents and family to The Hague and had a wonderful time. He remembers his first Eurovision adventure:

It was a fantastic experience, when we went to The Hague for the first time. My mum used to have a brother who was a really good musician. He's in America – he's a guitar player and singer. I can't sing, and can't really play the piano. My mother always used to say, 'Look at that fella there [me], he's going to break the piano, he hasn't a note in his head.' It was lovely that they and my wife Mary and the children came over. The eldest one was quite small at that time. I was thrilled, as Red gave a great performance, the song did very well here (it reached the top five), and I believe he still sings it. I'm only sorry that I did not give Red a better song. The other song, 'Jacqueline', came out shortly afterwards from DJ Curtin. He had a phenomenal voice. I remember having the radio on one day, and the next thing I knew I heard Larry Gogan saying, 'And now at number six, 'Jacqueline' by DJ Curtin.' I remember arriving home from The Hague on a Sunday. I had this out-of-tune, upright piano. I dropped my cases in the hall, and went straight to the piano. The way I looked at it was, 'OK, I've learnt something, but I need to do better. I need to get on and start working on the next song.' That afternoon, as soon as I got home, I went straight on and started working on something else. You did have the sense of occasion, and the sense of representing your country, which I think gets overlooked, but it's a huge thing, and that was my first Eurovision experience.

In 1977 Bill Whelan would have his first direct involvement with a Eurovision song. He explains how the process worked:

In those days the focus, at the early stages of the National Song Contest, was the song. People sent in songs. Nobody knew who was going to sing them, they just sent in the songs. There was a selection panel. I played piano, and we would be locked away for a week in the Montrose Hotel in Dublin. You could have five or six hundred songs that came in, in sheet music or tape and even acetate discs. Then you chose the songs, not on the basis of who was going to perform them, or what they were going to look like on the final night, but on the basis of whether they were good songs.

The panel would choose eight songs, with an overflow of maybe two or three, in case there were any problems with copyright, and so on. Twelve songs or so were chosen, and then the final eight went into the television show. It wasn't until that stage that the singer was chosen. That was normally done, I think, by Tom McGrath, or whoever was the producer of the show. They would go to the singers of the day – the Dickie Rocks, the Sonny Knowles, the Butch Moores. Managements would make representations to Tom and say, 'We have a great singer this year if you have a song for them in the NSC.' It was very democratic: everybody had to present a song the same way, with a live orchestra, so there were no production-value differences between the songs. The choice of the arranger was the next thing. The song first, the singer second and then the arranger. Then it was down to presentation. That was done as a kind of afterthought. Now, over the years that's probably been reversed completely [laughs]. Now it's all a production thing. In a funny kind of way, once the singer was chosen, they took over the song. The writer would then take a secondary position, and was often ignored (which was an annoyance for me, as a writer). I used to think: 'Hey! Why aren't they talking to the person who wrote the song?' It was a natural thing: the person presenting the song to the singer was the person everybody focused on. It was still about the song. As well as having to have the Irish song, it also had to be arranged by an Irish arranger, and it had to be written by an Irish national. It couldn't be done the way things are done now. In those days it was a very national thing.

More big names continued to take part annually. Dickie Rock returned to the National after eight years. The Swarbriggs returned for their third year in a row. Tommy Swarbrigg had a plan that time around:

In 1977 we deliberately wrote a song for the Eurovision that people would remember after one hearing. That was the criteria we set ourselves. Dana's brother Gerry Browne was in with a song that year. Chips had a great song; Colm

Wilkinson had a good song. When I heard the songs that we were up against, I knew that it is going to be a tough one. We were gobsmacked, and delighted to come out on top.

The Swarbriggs weren't alone this time. They were now The Swarbriggs Plus Two. Alma Carroll remembers:

> *I had been doing a bit of work with Tom McGrath on The Mike Murphy Show and The Likes of Mike, and things like that. He just said: 'Will you come in?' It was Tom who said: 'Look, the guys are great, the song is good, but I want to put two girls with them.' And that's what we did. So I was together with Nicola Kerr in the National Song Contest. I didn't even know Nicola at the time. We wore black and white dresses, Nicola and I, all matching, and the guys were in suits and white shirts. A man called Thomas Wolfangel made the dresses for us. When we won the NSC there was a lot of talk about the dresses. People were writing in saying, 'Don't change the dresses, wear them in the Eurovision.' We wore the same dresses for the Eurovision that we wore in the NSC. I'm was so pleased to have been involved in all those different NSCs, and then to actually win with Jimmy, Tommy and Nicola.*

Bill Whelan was brought on board to arrange his first Eurovision song for the London contest.

> I remember doing the arrangement. I remember getting the song. That was when I lived up in Dundrum. I remember bringing it into the house, sitting at the piano and working on the arrangement for 'It's Nice To Be in Love Again'. I remember writing that introduction to the song, and bringing them in, that was The Swarbriggs Plus Two, Nicola Kerr and Alma Carroll. I remember them all coming up to my house in Dundrum and rehearsing at the piano. That was the first one I did.

In London, The Swarbriggs used their past experience to great success. Tommy explains:

> The big thing we learned from 1975 was that you had to have a commercial song to be in with a fighting chance, which we did. 'That's What Friends Are For' just wasn't commercial enough. That's why, two years later, we wrote a song especially for the contest. You only get a chance to listen to the song a couple of times, so it's got to be commercial, and we went for it. RTÉ didn't pay for the arranger to come to the Eurovision Song Contest in those days, and Bill Whelan didn't have the money for the airfare to London, so we brought him over, that's a fact. He was only just married. He did a gorgeous job arranging the song, and he came with us, and he was a friend. The late Lindsey de Paul was a header. She didn't mix with anyone, but we had a great time anyway. It's a lottery, and you take what comes. We got great coverage out of it, and the song roamed around the lower regions of the charts in some European countries but at least it was being played. It made number one here in Ireland [knocking Abba off the top spot]. We were in London with our record company when we heard the news, and we had a wee glass of champagne. We sang first on the night, which is not a good position, but we did well, and finished third.

Alma Carroll remembers it fondly:

> It was a great experience, I remember we were first on that night, which was nerve-racking. We had the whole show to sit through before the results came in, but it was wonderful. That year we got the twelve votes from England, and we thought we were on our way. The woman is dead now, lord rest her, but Lyndsey de Paul didn't want to know about any of us. Even though we didn't win, I was thrilled that the French song won in the end and Lyndsey got wiped. She came second. 'Rock Bottom' was, to be fair, quite a good

song. It's a wonderful memory and I'm very proud to have done it. The only thing if I would have changed was our name. 'The Swarbriggs Plus Two' wasn't a great name.

By the time of the 1978 NSC, Bill Whelan was a member of the multi-talented Stacc, who played gigs around Dublin, including at the Merrion Inn. They were a musician's band, jazz-orientated, who performed original material as well as different arrangements of James Taylor, Paul Simon and Steely Dan numbers. They were part of that group of freelance musicians around Dublin who enjoyed playing together, and decided to form a band. Along with Bill, there was Des Moore on guitar, John Drummond on bass and Dessie Reynolds on drums. They were later joined by the aforementioned Nicola Kerr (who had been in Chips) and Catriona Walsh. This was the only time Bill would enter a song into the National, when 'All Fall Down', performed by Gemma Craven, would finish third. Stacc would finish second with the John Drummond composition 'You Put the Love in My Heart', Sheeba also made their debut in the event, as Maxi recalls:

> We had just formed, and went into rehearsals with Billy Browne for about three months. He was our musical director, God rest him. He wrote 'Amazing What Love Can Do'. Billy did all our harmonies. He didn't tour with us but he rehearsed with us and groomed us for recording. That was our first one as Sheeba, and Danny Doyle was in that year. Colm Wilkinson was breathtaking. That man, to this day, is fantastic. He walked on, walked off and won the whole thing. Even during rehearsals we were all saying, 'Oh my God'. The range of the man and his onstage presence was outstanding. He was a very popular winner. He's world-class. I was at school with the Wilkinsons (his sister was in my class), so I was thrilled for Colm. He absolutely deserved it.

One legendary Irish broadcaster attended his first Eurovision in Paris that year, and has fond memories of working with the late Terry Wogan. Larry Gogan explains:

1978 was the first one I did. Mike Murphy used to do all the commentaries. When he couldn't do it, Tom McGrath asked me to. Colm Wilkinson was singing. For that first one in Paris, they were doing it in French. I said to Terry, 'I haven't a word of French, and I don't know what they said.' 'I'll settle this,' he replied. He said, 'The Irish commentator and myself don't understand a word of French.' The languages of the Eurovision are English and French, so it has to be said in English as well as French. The French think everyone should know French. I remember there was no commentator there for Yugoslavia – that was before they broke up – and Terry (referring to me) said that the Irish commentator knew Yugoslavian perfectly. So they all turned to me and asked how it was pronounced. I had to to get up and say it as best I could. God knows what they thought. Oh, Terry was an awful man altogether. I remember another time we were in our commentary box, and it was very hot, and he'd shout down to me: 'Gogan, I have a fan!' But he was great craic.

CHAPTER FOUR

LOGAN'S RUN

As the decade drew to a close, the final NSC of the seventies would see the emergence of a man who would dominate it over the next fifteen years with numerous entries, not to mention several Eurovision successes. Johnny Logan remembers why he got involved:

> Red Hurley's brother and Tommy Hayden's brother had written this song called 'Angelina' for the Castlebar Song Contest. I came third with it. If you were a singer with showbands or if you played with a rock band, you either lived with your mother or went and lived in London with five or six guys. There was no real outlet for a rock band in Ireland; there really was no outlet at all in general. It was perfect for a middle-of-the-road singer or a showband singer. The only way to get outside of Ireland, to be known outside of Ireland, was through the Eurovision. It was the most direct way; it was the recognised way. The Eurovision was an outlet.
>
> I remember I'd started writing songs, and I'd written this song originally called 'Andy'. When it got into the National Song Contest, they asked me would I change the name because of the gay connotations, so I changed it to 'Angie'. I remember John Drummond did the arrangement for it, the bass player who also played on 'What's Another Year', and who I worked with many other times. 'Doodle' was his nickname, and he had the best moustache in the business. That song came third in the contest. It was my

first real experience in the National Song Contest, and it was a huge thing for me at the time.

Also taking part that year were past Eurovision representatives Red Hurley and Tina, who duetted on 'Hiding Behind Our Smile.' Other finalists included The Memories, Tweed, The Miami, and Catriona Walsh (Stacc), who would go on to top the Irish charts later that year with '*Viva il Papa*', her tribute to the visit of Pope John Paul II. She would also sing backing vocals for Ireland in Jerusalem.

Cathal Dunne was a Cork musician and a nephew of politician Jack Lynch. He'd been sending songs to the NSC from when he was about sixteen, and witnessed his first Eurovision Song Contest in Stockholm. While working in Sweden, he wrangled a ticket through RTÉ to see The Swarbriggs. He would come face to face with them the following year. His song 'Danny' made the final, but despite getting eight out of ten votes from Dublin, he received hardly any country votes, and finished fourth, behind Red Hurley. He was a qualified teacher, and by 1979 he was thinking of emigrating to Australia. Cathal remembers those tough times:

> Things were pretty bad in 1979, and the showband scene was dying, if not dead. If it was, we didn't realise it. We'd be working, for example, the next week, Friday, Saturday and Sunday, and then suddenly maybe Red Hurley or someone would be bounced from a top showband that would be a bigger draw than them. Then they'd call our place and they would move in because the promoter would make more money out of him than us, and suddenly we'd have no bookings at all. It was awful. There was guerrilla warfare taking place. It was an awful time. My aim was to win the National. I wrote the verse of the song going in on the train to Dublin, and I wrote the chorus in my flat in Monkstown. I was renting a basement flat for £45 a month. I believed in the song.
>
> At that point I hadn't heard the other songs, but I had studied the Eurovision enough to know that I had a very catchy chorus. The verse could have been stronger but the chorus was pretty good. I was still planning the day before that, still doing the showband thing. I had forty quid in my pocket, and I went to the bookies and put forty quid down to win. He gave me seven-to-one odds, and I won two hun-

dred and eighty quid. When he asked for my favourite and who I was, I told him I was Cathal Dunne. 'Cathal who?' I went in again three days later looking for the money, and he said, 'Ah go away you aul bollocks.' We had invitations in the post every morning in Dublin to the latest club, museum and so on.

We were beautiful people for a few months, and it was great, great craic. We did a few charities for Down's syndrome kids and they had a visual of a guy they were watching on television. That was magic. Television was way more powerful then. If you appeared on television in 1979 and won the National Song Contest, you were way up there, and people didn't think of you as human. I was in the loo in the National Ballroom and just about to do the show, and one guy said, 'Fuck it, you piss too'. The song was recorded in London, and then they gave me a publishing contract with a thousand paragraphs. I hadn't a clue what I was signing, and I signed the song away completely and never made a penny from it.

Cathal had been all over the world at festivals from Bulgaria to Tokyo, so was well travelled when he flew to Israel via London. When Cathal arrived in Tel Aviv he was brought to a hotel, where he was greeted by paparazzi and cameras. There was an amazing amount of security, which was why Noel Kelehan decided not to travel. He was nervous about travelling, so Frank Dunne deputised. Cathal remembers his Eurovision experience:

I was with a manager at the time who took the week in Jerusalem for sightseeing with his partner. On the day of the song contest, and after the rehearsal and so on, I was totally on my own. It was a tough old time. Normally when you're in that environment, you'd think there would be people with you, but there was nobody there. I didn't know where the three girls had gone, and it was pretty damn lonely. I took one hell of a double-brandy before I went out on stage. The biggest heartbreak was that, for a few minutes at the sound rehearsal, the final soundcheck, there was a little bit of a buzz. We were in the running. Did I think we were in the running? No, I had a reasonable song. Some of them were more show than song. I was managed by a fellow called Guy Robinson and he came in with fifteen telegrams with invitations to all the top TV shows – *Top of the Pops*, shows in France and Switzerland – if we won. In five minutes, that was all gone. That was the hardest thing, to be so close.

One thing that gets overlooked regarding Israel's win in 1979, and was possibly a crucial element in their success, was something that had nothing at all to do with music. The week of the contest, Israeli Prime Minister Menachem Begin and Egyptian President Anwar Sadat signed a peace treaty, witnessed by US President Jimmy Carter. Cathal continues:

It was pretty huge that, just around the corner in Jerusalem, a peace treaty had been signed. Everybody was delighted, and I think that helped them. Do I think I was robbed? Absolutely not! Do I think the winning song is a better song? Absolutely yes! I think 'Hallelujah' is a terrific song, but it broke my heart. I would have picked that one too, had I been judging. I have no hard feelings but, looking back, I think there was a little bias towards them because of that particular event. That was a much more important event in Jerusalem than the Eurovision. In fairness to RTÉ, they brought us out to Bethlehem and the Wailing Wall, and they were very kind. Tom McGrath was a bit of a bully. He was the head honcho and we had to toe the line, but at the end of the concert, when we didn't win, he said, 'You did Ireland proud. Not alone for the television, but for the week that you were here. You never got drunk, everybody liked you and you were well received'. I appreciated that. We won the National, but I wasn't confident and possibly wasn't ready for the Eurovision.

After finishing third at both the Castlebar and the NSCs in 1979, Johnny Logan recalls meeting Shay Healy around this time:

It was at the Castlebar Song Contest that I met Shay Healy, and he said to me: 'I have a song that I'm putting in for the

National Song Contest, and if I get it in, will you sing it for me?' It was 'What's Another Year'. When I first heard it, it was a country song. Then Bill Whelan got his hands on it, and turned it into what it is now.

Shay recalls that meeting with Johnny only too well:

It was at the Castlebar Song Contest that I really saw Johnny Logan up close for the first time. I'd seen him in a musical in the State Theatre earlier that year, and he was a big lump of a young guy, very handsome, and I asked him if he would sing for me. He agreed that he would, and then he drove me home to Dublin. By the time we got home I said, 'I still want you to sing my song in the National Song Contest, but I'm never getting in a car with you again.' He was a rally driver. That was the first time I met Johnny and got to know his character. The next thing was that we had to do an arrangement of the song and, very fortunately, Bill Whelan had come to town a couple of years earlier. I asked him if he'd arrange the song, and he came back with a beautiful arrangement that was very moveable. He transformed the song and Johnny Logan sang it, and we thought, there's something very special here, it could go a long way.

Bill Whelan remembers working on the arrangement:

Very interestingly, I had been working with that sax player Colin Tully on something else, and I said to Shay, a sax solo in the middle of this song would be great, and then I wrote that key change for the sax to go into it, and then back into the song again, and I was really proud of it and liked it, and Shay was wonderful to work with, as was Johnny.

Shay recalls writing the song some years previously:

I was with Spotlight in 1970 when Dana won, and I went to America in 1971. I missed 'Cross Your Heart' and all of them. I came back in 1975. In November I was in town taking a bus back out. I lived in Blackrock at the time, and there were two kids sitting upstairs on the bus. One of them said 'What's Another Year', and that caught me. I got off the bus and walked, and by the time I'd got to my front door I had all the verses, but not the middle. It was 1979 before I wrote the middle piece for it. I went in with Jim O Neill,(the radio DJ), and the late John Brady, into Lombard Studios, and we put down a mid-tempo country ballad. Carolyn Fisher, the PA officer, rang me and said, 'You're in, you're in, you're in! You're in the National Song Contest!' I thought, we have a chance here. There were seven other songs, but there was one song, 'Stepping Stones' by Peter Beckett. He was just behind me. I remember getting full points from Wexford, and knowing then that I was home and dry. It was a great feeling.

Johnny concurs with being grateful to Wexford:

I'll always be grateful to Wexford. I remember when the voting came in it was very close until they got to Wexford. Wexford gave me all twelve points, and that ended any competition.

With Israel's consecutive victories at the end of the seventies, and the 1980 event scheduled for 19 April (a national holy day in Israel), they opted not to stage it, and withdrew from the event. The Hague took the honour of once more staging the contest. Shay Healy remembers it fondly:

We didn't know the rules of how you support yourself during the week of the Eurovision, but the Turkish delegation were staying at the same hotel as us, and we struck up a tremendous rapport with them. My wife Didi became good friends with their singer Ajda, and every night we had a great sing-song at the piano and Andy O'Callaghan was magnificent. He played everything you could think of, and we sang every night until 4 or 5 AM in the morning. All the different delegations partied all week; we constantly had the craic. Then we went into Amsterdam one night with Pat Kenny at the wheel and he took us the wrong way down a one-way street and the police escorted us back to the hotel. For the twenty-fifth anniversary of our win I went looking for Colin Tully, the guy who played saxophone on 'What's Another Year'. I tracked him down to a music school in Wales eventually. I asked him what he remembered, and he told me, 'Do you remember the night before the concert we went to Amsterdam?' I said I did, and he said, 'Well whatever I smoked that night, I thought I was going to die, and when I woke up the next morning and I was still alive, I never played as well in my life.'

Johnny was more concerned with the job in hand:

I'd never been outside of Ireland on my own, and everything was new. It was completely overwhelming and I felt like a little boy lost in it all. Maybe that's part of the reason I won, because maybe that's what came across in the performance. I was the third favourite when I arrived over in The Hague, and then I disappeared from the top ten, and got back in when I won. I didn't pay that much attention to it. To be honest I was more interested trying to get a look at people who were stars and who weren't stars. I was just star-spotting. One thing that sticks in my head was, when I arrived and I was waiting for my bags, I saw Thomas Ledin, who was a backing vocalist and a huge artist in Sweden. He was with Stig Anderson (Abba's manager), and his daughter was managing him. There was an army of photographers around him as he went by, and I managed to grab my bag and saw them all marching by because he was a huge star. When I left The Hague, I remember seeing him sitting waiting to board his flight, and there were racks of photographers around me, photographing me. It was an awful lot to contend with in those days.

Shay remembers the build-up to the big night:

> What happens is that you tend to go along and listen to other people's rehearsals to see what the opposition is like, and the more you hear it, the more you see it, the more confused you become. I was very scared of the Italian guy [Alan Sorrenti]. He had a lovely song. He was a smooth-looking geezer, who wore lovely clothes. I thought he could be a problem, but someone told me that his wife had threatened to throw herself out a window. I thought to myself, that's him fucked. In the end, the voting was close enough that it was made very interesting. My only regret is that there was a big white balustrade that ran from where we were near the balcony all the way down to the stage. I was just disgusted that I didn't have enough panache to put my arse on it and slide the whole way down.

It may have been his first Eurovision, but Johnny did something that even the most experienced act there on the night wouldn't have thought of:

> They were all putting their make-up on beforehand and getting ready for the show. It seems to be a trend in my life, when I go to do something big, to react in an intelligent way. It's probably the only time that I do. I was very aware of where the cameras were at rehersals. I went out to the stage to watch the people coming in. I didn't want it all to be new to me when I went out on the stage. I wanted to be familiar with what I was going to see when I came out. I also went downstairs with Colin Tully, to a little locker room. I sang 'Danny Boy', and he played the saxophone on it. We did a load of Irish songs for each other, and sang and played to each other. Then we went upstairs, and won the song contest.

Shay recalls the mixed emotions afterwards:

I had a sweatshirt with 'It is imperative that I win this contest', and I wore it all week. When I finally won on the night, I got a pen and I wrote, 'It is no longer imperative that I win this contest'. When I won, I was out in the auditorium where all the other writers were. I was in a fetal position saying 'Oh no, oh no'. When I won I stood up and stretched my arms out, and my pal Roy Esmond captured that moment. I still have the picture. I was delighted with Johnny's performance on the night. He was flawless. We both got a trophy. Johnny got one and I got one, in that order. The crowd clamoured for the singer, while the songwriters were treated like muck. So I sneaked off on my own, and said I'd go to the hotel across the square, where the media had a room booked for a picture party. I was on my own with my trophy and my blazer. I never felt such contempt in my whole life. As I walked across that square, a complete calm came over me. I bumped into Pat Kenny and Grainne O'Connor, who I'd met on the way back. We just sat down at the side of the road and laughed, and laughed and laughed. That was my reaction to it. When I got to the hotel I went downstairs to the room where the event was taking place. There were slots for the names of the contestants. Some of the contestants' names had been thrown on the floor. Only Johnny Logan's remained. That's how cold the contest is: it only respects the winner.

If the Eurovision only had respect for the winning songwriter that evening, there was one man back in Dublin who held Shay in the highest regard possible. Bill Whelan remembers that night vividly:

Unfortunately I couldn't go to the Eurovision, as I was working with Planxty. I was in the studio and we were down to the wire to finish a recording. I had Andy Irvine and Donal Lunny with me. We asked the tape operators and assistant engineer if they could go to the green room and let us know what's happening. So we went out for the performance and then came back in. We asked them to keep an eye on the voting and to let us know what's going on. The next minute, one of the lads came running in and said it looked like we were gonna win this thing, so we all left the studio and watched, and it was phenomenal. I can't tell you what it was like, the feeling of being there, seeing them win, and seeing Shay and Johnny. We'd become good friends by that stage. It was a great moment and I'll never forget it. We turned off the television and went back into the studio. My mother was very ill in the Mater Hospital at the time. The phone rang within five minutes of the end of the broadcast, and it was my mother. She had asked the nurse to ring me to say, 'Congratulations, you're on your way', but about a minute later. You've got to put this in the context of 1980s technology – there was no such thing as a mobile phone. A minute later, I had Shay Healy on the phone. He said thanks, and that he wished we were there. We shared the moment and it was fantastic, for the winner of the Eurovision to have found his way to a phone and to call Windmill Lane Studios. There was a massive reception at Dublin when he came home. After all the fuss and press and everything, Shay got into the limo and pulled into the Mater Hospital on his way back with a magnum of champagne for my mother. I will never forget Shay for that. It's the personal things that go on behind the Eurovision that you remember most.

Johnny also remembers the homecoming:

We were supposed to do a press conference. I arrived and couldn't believe the amount of people that were there. Instead of going through passport control I saw them outside. I just wanted to be with the people, so I just pushed the door open and went out. Suddenly I was in the middle of thousands of people. The police surrounded me and decided to put me in a limousine. I couldn't get back into the airport, so they held the press conference without me. I have a huge wall-size photograph of that homecoming.

Shay has very fond memories of also returning home a hero:

We had a homecoming at Dublin Airport. I was the acting press and information executive for RTÉ at the time that we won, so I had to hold a press conference for myself. The mob was all the way along the balcony and down to the tarmac. It was brilliant. Johnny came out and there was pushing and shoving, and then my da and my kids, and then someone from RTÉ, said, 'We have a car for you outside.' It was a big car, not quite a limo, but I laughed again and thought, fuck me, RTÉ are giving me a limo. Unfortunately my wife had run into a glass door at Schipol Airport and badly cut her head, so we decided we had to go to A&E. We stopped at Madigan's in Donnybrook on the way, which had been our local pub for all those years in RTÉ. I remember walking through the door, and the whole pub stood up and gave me a standing ovation, and that was a special moment for me. My dad told me that after the contest, himself and his brother, my uncle Tom, had gone out to O'Reilly's Pub in Sandymount. When they walked through the door they got a standing ovation as well. That night there was a party for us out in the Country Club in Portmarnock. The Eurovision was on a Saturday night, and on the Friday night J. R. Ewing had been shot. It was one of the first big screens in Dublin, and on the big screen they had J.R. being shot in Dallas, and Johnny Logan wins Eurovision, and J. R. being shot in Dallas ,and Johnny Logan winning Eurovision. They had all that on a loop all night. Two big coups in one go.

Louis Walsh reflects on his Eurovision adventure:

I didn't know that it was going to win at all. It was a very ordinary demo, but Bill Whelan did what the man does best, and put in that sax solo. It was so different, and the song went to The Hague and changed everything for Johnny. I was very young and very naive about the business, but it was a brilliant time. I remember coming back to Dublin Airport and it was like Beatlemania, there were thousands of people there, and the banners and flags were brilliant. It was a massive, massive time. Then it was number one in Ireland and England and I got to do *Top of the Pops* with him. That kind of opened my mind to the whole business outside of Ireland, because I went away to do the television shows all over Europe, and he was just a proper pop star and I think he was great in all the countries he went to, and was a great ambassador for Ireland.

For Shay and Johnny, the world was their oyster, and the opportunity was there to tour and promote the song. As Louis mentioned, Johnny remembers one legendary music show:

> I've done *Top of the Pops* fourteen times. In those days you did it live, with an orchestra and everything. There was the studio the orchestra were sitting in, and you sang, and the saxophone was played live by Colin Tully. I went to number one and they gave me a cake on the show. It was the day of my birthday and they gave me a twenty-sixth birthday cake.

Shay fondly remembers his song topping the charts:

> I remember waking up in the Kensington Hilton Hotel, and a guy on the television said that 'What's Another Year', the song that won the Eurovision, had gone to number one today in the UK charts. It was about ten to seven in the morning, and I just lay there for a couple of hours and let it sink in. We were number one for two weeks, and then were knocked out by the theme from *M*A*S*H*, and it was the last Eurovision-winning song to go to number one in eleven countries.

To mark the twenty-fifth anniversary of his win, on 19 April 2005, Shay met up with backing singers Rita Madigan, Pat Reilly and the late Anne Bushnell outside the Abbey Theatre and called a cab. The three ladies got into the back and Shay sat beside the driver.

When Shay explained to the driver that he had some valuable cargo in the back, the taxi driver started singing 'I've been waiting, such a long time...'. As they drove across town, Rita, Pat and Anne sang all the backing vocals once more. In the past few years, Shay has sung the song himself, as he explains:

> It's kind of mad. In the last few years I've done some small
> gigs in tiny pubs. I'd never sung it in public, but I've
> performed it about seven or eight times now in places like
> the concert hall in Limerick and in the Sugar Club. It stops
> traffic every time.

The Eurovision was back in Ireland for the second time, and there was a renewed interest in it. Tony Kenny returned with the Brendan Graham composition 'Can't Be Without You', and Nicola Kerr was solo with 'The One in My Life'. Sheeba were back again, and Bill Whelan recalls being involved:

> At that stage I had done quite a bit of work as an arranger,
> and I was getting more and more freelance work from it. I
> was brought in often, and would sit at the sound desk with
> Willie O'Reilly and read the scores. I was the link, from a mu-
> sical perspective, between Noel Kelehan and the production
> team. I would audition many of the singers. There was a job
> there called 'Music Associate'. I was the general overseer of
> all aspects of the show to do with music, and I liaised with
> the orchestra.

Making their debut appearance in the NSC that year were The Duskeys. Sandy Kelly recalls:

> Somebody approached us with the song 'Where Does That
> Love Come From'. I think it was written by Red Hurley's
> brother Liam. At the time The Nolan Sisters were huge. We
> kind of fancied ourselves as that sort of thing, so that's
> probably where that concept and that idea all came from.
> That was the first year we did it, and we didn't even expect
> to come third. It whet our appetite. We were on the road
> about six or seven nights a week, doing what we were doing
> reasonably successfully. We got a lot of experience, given that
> we started as kids, really. We were very focused about it. I

think we felt, when we went to the National Song Contest that year, that the powers-that-be tried to change us. We were brought into Dublin and given free haircuts and suits. It wasn't us. Coming up to the competition, we didn't feel comfortable. It wasn't about the song – we just didn't feel that the costumes were what we'd normally wear. We didn't feel that the choreographer that was brought in was 'us', or that the hair was 'us'. We came third, which we thought was very good. We said, 'Do you know what we're gonna do? We're gonna go away, and if we get this chance next year, we're gonna do it our way.' We were as well prepared as you could be, but not as us. You have to be yourself.

Three years on from their sixth-place finish, Sheeba were successful that time round, something Maxi remembers very well:

We had done work in Spain, France and Germany as Sheeba. Billy Browne had lots of connections, and we had been sent away and were all very experienced anyway. Marion Fossett was with Fossett's Circus. As she says, she was on the back of an elephant when she was still in the womb. Frances Campbell was also a very experienced singer in the north. The National Song Contest in '81 was held in RTÉ, and that was the year after Johnny had won. Winning the National that year was very special, because Johnny had won and coming home, and it was lovely to be the Irish representative.

Celebrating its two hundred and fifteenth anniversary, the RDS (Royal Dublin Society) was chosen as the venue for the twenty-sixth Eurovision, and Ian McGarry was chosen as the producer and director. Ian had originally being involved in the 1968 NSC, playing drums as part of the RTÉ Light Orchestra. As previously mentioned, he was working as a TV cameraman by 1971. He later moved into producing and directing, and would be the man responsible for changing the name from the NSC to the Eurosong. Ian remembers '81:

Tom McGrath continued to do the NSC, as far as I remember, up till about '81 or '82. In 1981 Noel Breen was the executive producer, and I was the producer/director. I had total control of the show itself. We decided that everything inside the four walls of the RDS in Ballsbridge was my responsibility, and that everything outside that was Noel's responsibility. And that was where I employed Bill Whelan to do the music, which we called 'Timedance'. That was prerecorded in Studio 1 in the Television Centre with Anne Courtney, who was the choreographer. Moya and John took the idea years later and called it *Riverdance*, so if you listen to the music of 'Timedance', it's a similar type of thing to *Riverdance*. We were over ten years too early and we didn't have Michael Flatley, the one thing lacking in '81. I think we were the first of the big shows. Up until then it hadn't been anything like the scale that we did in the RDS. Now you look at it today and it's a vast production. We were one of the first stations to do a big production of the show. It had been relatively big before, but given the size of the RDS, it's fair to say we brought it up a notch. That's the plan every year, to make it bigger and better.

Maxi was proud to be the home representative:

I always look on the good and the bouncy side of things, and we were absolutely delighted to be the host country, and all that it entailed. Because we were the host, we met the other contestants and welcomed them, answered their questions: 'Where can I buy an Aran sweater? Where can I get an Irish whiskey?' The culture of Ireland came into it big-time then, so we were approachable and we had a few good years under our belt as Sheeba, so we knew that the public-relations part of it was very, very important for Ireland, and we were honoured to be there, and they would also knock on your door and say, 'I was wondering if you would say this or that for me in Irish', and so we began to realise how vast the Eurovision stretched. The girls were always saying to me because I had the experience of '73 under my belt, they would come to me for advice about the public-relations work that is part of your win, so, not so much Marion, because she had the experience of the circus, but Frances hadn't, and she's say, 'Oh, what's this for?' and you'd say, 'Oh, you're probably going to be asked who's gonna win the Grand National', and you don't have to study horses, you just have to give an answer. PR stuff. It's like people ring you and say what's your memory of X, Y and Z. Give an intelligent, funny answer if you can, but those little interviews were part of your day. The interval act was 'Timedance' by Bill Whelan with Planxty. There's a sensation you get when you see beauty and hear beauty like that, and it was very special. It was the precursor to *Riverdance*.

Christy Moore was part of the interval performance:

It was a truly memorable experience. Planxty played 'Timedance' for the Irish Ballet Company, and two hundred million people went to their kitchens to make tea. The seed for *Riverdance* was sown, and I got to bang my *bodhrán* for ballerinas. Jaysus, if we'd have had [Michael] Flatley as well, we'd all be fartin' through silk.

Bill remembers his first Eurovision interval piece:

Donal Lunny and I wrote 'Timedance' between us. There were three pieces. One was a traditional piece for which Liam played the pipes, and then there was a piece that I had written in Galway. It was called 'Isercleran', named after the house I wrote it in. Then there was a piece by Donal that was called 'The Ballymun Regatta'. We put the three of them together, and Donal and I did the arrangement – I did the orchestral arrangement. It became a single for Planxty, and Planxty signed to Warner on the strength of that. It was an extraordinary time to be involved, and the reason I called it *Riverdance* was to make the connection with 'Timedance'. In many ways, even though 'Timedance' wasn't an Irish dance, it was a ballet. I wanted to make the connection.

Mike Nolan was born in Dublin, as were most of his brothers. Originally from Finglas, the Nolans moved to Crumlin, before moving to the UK when he was four. By 1980, Mike had been in several groups and wanted to try his hand at a solo career. With Mike's help, Nichola Martin submitted the song 'Making Your Mind Up'. When it was selected for the UK national final, she asked Mike to join the group to sing it, saying, 'It'll never win anyway.' Mike reluctantly agreed to join the group, and she advertised for three other people. The only stipulation was that they had to be no taller than five foot seven inches (Mike's height). Mike recalls the formation of the group:

> When Nichola was putting the group together, she was looking for another girl, but she was dying to be in it herself. She felt that she was too old to be in the group, so she found Cheryl and Jay during the auditions, and said, 'I'm definitely not going to be in this group.' Then she found Bobby. We all met up one Sunday. I knew I was going to be in the group, as she'd already spoken to me about it. When I got there, we were sat down and told: 'For the next three months you are now known as Bucks Fizz. Grow to like each other and let's get on with the work.' Everyone sat around watching everyone rehearse in the national final, and as soon as we got up to perform, everyone turned around and said we might as well go home now because we'd won it. We all felt that we were going to win it. It was between us and a band called Liquid Gold. 'Making Your Mind Up' is not a brilliant song, but the routine made it good. Everyone remembered those skirts being ripped off.

Cheryl Baker would go on to marry the bass guitarist of Beyond, one of the other UK finalists that night. She had horrible memories of her previous Eurovision experience with Coco in 1978. Dublin was much better, as it was much more casual, and the people were a lot friendlier to her and the band. Mike remembers everything about Dublin:

We got there on the Tuesday and left on the Sunday after the contest. I remember the whole week, everything I did, and the memory of it never ever left us. I remember meeting up with my family over there. I had evenings off, and I'd go over and see them all. They were so excited. They backed the UK instead of Ireland for the first time ever, because they wanted us to win. My mum's family came up from Cork to join my dad's family. They all went to a hotel that night. I had no money, but I bought a case of champagne and put it in the room for them. They didn't touch it till before the voting finished. The only people that went that night were a friend of mine and my dad. My mum was supposed to go, but she was so nervous it had made her ill. She decided to stay in the hotel with the family. Both my parents are now deceased, but if you watch it, the camera goes out into the audience, and you can actually see my dad. He's rather tall, and was waving his hands in the air. He broke through all the security and managed to get in at the back. We could hear him shouting 'Michael, Michael', and Cheryl was going, 'Is that not your dad?' He eventually broke through the crowd of photographers, and jumped up to where the reception was, and threw his arms around all of us. He was so excited. I think my family were mad moving from Ireland to the UK. I often say to the girls, though, that 'If I'd have never moved over here, we'd never have won the Eurovision.' They'd ask, 'What do you mean?' and I would reply, 'Well, Ireland gave us ten points because I was in the band.' If I hadn't been in the band it wouldn't have worked.

Sheeba would finish fifth, with 'Horoscopes', another compositon by Joe Burkett. Joe had written several previous NSC entrants, including 'Give Me All Your Love' (Alma Carroll), 'Too Late' (Butch Moore), 'The Sad Sound' (Des Smyth) and *'Ceol An Ghrá'* in 1972. Maxi became friends with Mike, a friendship that continues to this day. She had no complaints that the best song won:

Bucks Fizz was absolutely the standout song. They had that trick with the skirts that was very, very clever. One must remember that some of the voters speak the language and some of them don't, and it's very important to go with striking visuals. It was very catchy, and epitomised youth and fun. They deserved to win. I admire creativity. You didn't have to speak English to smile when that happened.

Shay Healy returned to hand over the songwriter's prize:

> I had Paddy Sweeney make me a jacket with bank bags in bright yellow, lime green, purple and pink. It was fantastic, and I enjoyed wearing it. I played a kind of ambassadorial role for the media, and when Bucks Fizz won, I spotted a blonde girl called Nichola Martin. She had put Bucks Fizz together. She herself sang in Bucks Fizz, but she put Jay Aston in her place. She was married to a guy called Andy Hill, who wrote the song. Some girl ran away with her husband the day after, and amidst all the hullabaloo backstage I said to her, 'I know what you're thinking, you're regretting that you gave up your slot.' She said, 'You're right.'

One RTÉ employee has a special memento from that night. Tommy Nolan explains:

> I only joined RTÉ in 1978, and was a stagehand in 1981. I think Mick Grogan was the designer. I worked with Noel D. Green in Strand Electrical before that, and he went on to bigger things in RTÉ [He became the executive producer.] The scoreboards were entirely manual. One of our guys was put in charge of putting them up. Our job was to clear the stage. I got the green dress – I didn't drag it off her. I have it in my house somewhere. I must ask the wife about that.

The NSC in 1982 had a feeling of déjà vu about it. Three of the acts from the previous year were back again: Tony Kenny, The Duskeys and Sheeba. Chips made what would be their final appearance. Linda Martin recalls that song:

I hate that song ['Tissue of Lies']. I'll be honest with you, that's probably the least favourite. Looking back on it now, it was rubbish. Dana's brother's song 'We Can Fly' was a jolly song. You could have fun with it. But that bloody 'Tissue of Lies' did my head in.

Paul Lyttle had a different opinion but wasn't impressed with the finished version:

We came last with 'Tissue of Lies'. It was one of the songs I was proudest of, and one of the songs that suffered from being orchestrated. It was meant to be a smoky type of song, with big acoustic guitars, drums and bass. But we got the full twenty-four-piece brass section, thirty-piece string section and the kitchen sink, and it killed it stone dead. Also it was the year after Bucks Fizz won, and it was suggested that we get rid of the instruments and stand and do the song à la Bucks Fizz, with two girls and two fellas, which was nothing to do with Chips. RTÉ suggested this and we went for it. The second fella wasn't even a singer, he was a friend of ours who was a dancer friend, and held us together for the silly movements we did. I followed what I was told to do; I lost all my integrity. It was their show. When you submit your song it becomes their property, and ceases to be yours until you've won or lost. We got some fame out of it because Gerry Ryan, Lord rest him, made it one of his worst Eurovision moments.

Maxi was more impressed with Sheeba's entry:

I thought '*Go Raibh Maith Agat*' was a beautiful song and that its verses were stunning. It was a very beautiful song, but if there are eight songs in a final, one song wins, seven songs don't, and that's it. We loved the song, we choreographed it and Billy Browne arranged it, and I'm really proud of that. It has beautiful polished harmonies. It depends on what your taste is.

But even Sheeba, with their experience behind them, were unable to beat The Duskeys, who still consisted of Sandy Kelly, her sister Barbara and cousin Nina. Now they had been joined by her cousin Simon. Sandy recalls:

> Dick Keating asked us to sing his song 'Here Today Gone Tomorrow'. We said OK, and very much kept it for the National Song Contest. We lost control for the Eurovision, but we kept the NSC in our own control. We dressed the way we wanted and did our own dance routine, and we won it. Dick Keating was one of the regular RTÉ musicians on the piano. He might have been with the orchestra. Dick Keating worked in RTÉ. I think that it was Dick who wrote the song. He may have entered another song, but he entered that song under his wife's name, Sally, who wasn't really in the music business.

Mike Murphy was back again to compère the event. Sandy was surprised that they won:

> With all respect to Dick and Sally, who I adore, it wasn't a very good song. We didn't expect to win the National Song Contest at all, but gave it our best shot in terms of dancing, costumes and our projection of ourselves. I think that's what won it. We were totally shocked. We went in there just giving it our best. The year before, we weren't happy going into it. We were very happy performing, as we didn't expect to win. When we went in to record the demo for Dick Keating, my second child had just been born. She was in hospital when we won the National Song Contest, with a cyst on her brain. That meant that, while we were performing at the Eurovision, she was actually at St Vincent's Hospital in Dublin having undergone brain surgery. We didn't expect to win. RTÉ had a big party for the winners, with music in the canteen and food and drink. Our manager Tom Kelly had actually taken a booking for us in the National Ballroom because no one thought we'd win. The first song we did was 'Here Today Gone Tomorrow', and then we were stars for eight weeks. Nobody was prepared for it, and no-

body thought we were going to win. We went straight into a recording studio in Dublin and recorded an entire album in two days. We slept on the floor of the studio, Crashed Records, with Shay Hennessey. Shay put together a whole album for The Duskeys, and within a week of the album being out, Anglo Irish Airways, who are no longer around, were flying us to all the airports around Ireland for press receptions. We were Abba for eight weeks.

Harrogate was a surprise choice of location for the Eurovision in 1982, but Sandy went there with her mind on personal matters. As she recalls:

When we went off to the Eurovision my daughter was very ill. I was seen as the leader of the group at that time, so I couldn't let them down. We didn't expect to win, and we didn't. We came tenth, which we thought was awful. By today's standards it isn't that bad, and Nicole was always the one to beat. We got so many bouquets of flowers coming back from the UK. Even complete strangers had bouquets for us. We brought them back to my daughter in hospital. The press at the time focused on my daughter being in hospital, and whether I would be able to perform and sing. I look back now and wonder, what the hell was I thinking? I said to myself that she was with family, she's had her operation, I was only going to be flying out for four days, and I wasn't letting anybody down. It wasn't a glory thing, because we knew we weren't going to win. It was a matter of representing your country and getting on with the job. When I think back, though, part of me thinks 'I chose it', but another part of me thinks, 'What was I doing?'

Before their Eurovision performance, The Duskeys had to film a postcard for the event, something Sandy now looks back at with a sense of humour:

Sheeba had been driven around all the designer places in Dublin in a limousine in fur coats. For us they turned up with a van, four pairs of wellies and dungarees. We were brought to the zoo to get out the elephants and give fish to the seals. That was typical of what used to happen to The Duskeys at the time. I always said the song was called 'Here Today Gone Tomorrow', and we were. We went there and had the best time. The late Anne Bushnell was one of the backing singers, who used to do the tributes to Edith Piaf, and Ian McGarry and Paul Clarke were with us. We went to every party and got on well with everybody. We loved every minute of it, because we weren't full of ourselves and because we had done the best job we could, even thought we knew we weren't going to win.

The buildup to the show was chaotic, as Sandy recalls:

We lost control when we got to the Eurovision. RTÉ picked someone to design the suits, and we hated them, but we did what we were told, and then when we got there, on the day of the Eurovision, my sister had to go out shopping for shoes with some of the people that were dressing us, and she ended up singing and dancing in the Eurovision with a pair of shoes that were a size too big for her, and we were telling them the whole time that we didn't like the costumes, but they wouldn't listen, and after the dress rehearsal we were called to an emergency meeting with the RTÉ staff to say that they didn't like the costumes, and we said, 'Well we told you that', they were these green catsuits, and you wouldn't have seen the top of it. Originally there was a blouse thing over the top of it with all sequins, so when the introduction music for the Eurovision was coming on (because we were second-last on), we were down in the basement of the Harrogate centre in the costume department, where they had taken the tops off us, and the sequins off the tops, and they were still working on them as the show was half over before we were sewn back into the suits to go back up and sing. Those kind of things unnerve you. Sometimes you have to go with your gut feeling if you're uncomfortable.

Sandy knew from the outset Germany were the favourites and Nicole was the one to beat:

It was obvious in rehearsals and it was obvious from her demeanour. Everybody else went to the party to socialise with other countries; she was kept completely apart from all of us. She never attended any of the functions. They were serious about winning. When she won it, she came out and sang it in every language. There should be a certain element of fun in the Eurovision. Back then there was, but now there isn't.   I
remember in the dress rehearsal how her producer went crazy after the make-up artist did her make-up. It had to be taken off her, as they wanted her to look young. It worked for them. All I know is that we had a much better time than she had.

Just like Shay Healy had experienced two years previously, it seemed the winner was the only one that mattered, as Sandy explains:

> One thing I do remember was that the hotel had all the flags up, but when we came back, all the losing flags had been taken down. These are the things that stick in your head. At our tables there had been the Irish flags, and the next morning at breakfast there was nothing. We had an absolute balll, and everybody was so nice. It's a great thing to say you did it. I would have liked to have gone back with the big ballad and had another whack at it. The whole experience was much better than I ever expected. I could have done without the wellies and mucking out the elephants, and I could have done with going to Cyprus instead of Yorkshire, but it was great fun.

Over thirty years on, Sandy still continues to perform, having recently toured Ireland and the UK. She also appeared in the country musical *Gotta Make That Train*. Her son Willie is a member of Rackhouse Pilfer, who performed with Imelda May on the most recent Tom Jones album.

In 1983, due to financial difficulties, RTÉ didn't hold a NSC, and thus Ireland missed out on competing in their first Eurovision since 1965, as Larry Gogan recalls:

> It was a financial thing. I remember Fred O'Donovan was the chairman of the authority, and he said we couldn't do it, we couldn't afford to spend the money on it, and nobody went.

Sadly, I always felt that one of the greatest Irish songs of all time, 'Edge of the Universe', written by Shay Healy and sung by Linda Martin, would surely have been a strong contender for victory in Munich that year. Linda would get her chance in the Eurovision the following year, and Shay had to be content with winning the Castlebar Song Contest with it. Sandy Kelly was certainly unaware that there were financial issues in RTÉ the following year. She concludes:

> I don't remember that. Oh Christ! Maybe we were to blame. They certainly didn't spend it on our suits.

RTÉ regrouped in 1984, after a year in the wilderness. Sheeba were back again and Linda Martin was now solo. Charlie McGettigan remembers his first NSC final:

> I remember Rob Strong being there. Aileen Pringle, the girl that did the backing vocals on the Eurovision Winners' Tour in 2012, was there that year also, and Sheeba. It became, not so much a club, but there was a lot of fierce goodwill when we'd all be out there together and everybody would know everybody. Everybody sent each other cards, and it was just a lovely, lovely experience. We were so lucky in those days, the amount of television and radio we got. There was so much more variety television then, when we were in it, and you were up and down, and you were doing *The Kelly Show*, and shows down here like afternoon shows. There were great places for music to be played, but now there's not.

Maxi remembers this NSC fondly too:

Our 1984 song 'My Love and You' was very close to my heart, as I co-wrote it. It was also my first time co-writing. Denis Woods was our piano player, and Denis and I used to write songs together. We came up with 'My Love and You', got it through, and decided to sing it ourselves. That was a very important year for me. It was the first time I became interested in co-writing.

Linda Martin was back in the final, this time as a solo artist. She explains how it happened:

Louis [Walsh] was managing Johnny at that stage. He'd been in our office from the late seventies. Johnny had won in 1980, and Louis still looked after him. We were all good buddies. He came up with 'Terminal 3'. At that stage Tom McGrath was very much still in control, and the song went through. I remember Tom ringing me and saying, 'Linda, come out to RTÉ. I want a word with you.' I went over and he said, 'I want you to listen to this song.' It was 'Terminal 3'. I already knew the song, and he said, 'I would like you to sing that in the National Song Contest. Would you be interested?' I said that of course I'd love to. That's how it was done. To win was just so brilliant.

Johnny remembers writing this one:

I wrote the guts of 'Terminal 3', the verses, in about 1982. I was at the airport in Heathrow, living in England at the time. In those days in London there was only terminal one, two and three, and I was waiting for my mother to come in from Australia. All the flight information was going up on the board, and I had this idea for a song. I got the verse, which led to another. I played it to Paul Lyttle from Chips a few years later, and Louis Walsh was looking for a song. A lot of it was down to Louis: he was always looking for songs. I said that I had this one. I played it, and it wasn't finished. I wrote the middle eight for it, the bridge section. To me that song was never finished, I was never happy with the middle part, and I think that's where it was let down, but it was only beaten on the last vote, which was amazing. I was quite shocked – I never thought it would get that far. I was sitting in the audience in shock. Shay Healy said to me afterwards, he was more aware of what was happening than I was.

Linda went to Luxembourg with high hopes of an Irish victory, and remembers her time there:

> Luxembourg is a very beautiful city, but there was not much to do at that stage. I remember that we were in a hotel with a piano and a bar, and the Irish delegation, which was huge at that stage. I think there were about thirty of us, between people joining us and people being employed by RTÉ. There was a bit of money at that stage. We had a photographer and all sorts of things. We certainly had a super time throughout that week, mainly because of the bar and the piano.

Also in Luxembourg, and commentating for TV for the last time, was a busy Gay Byrne:

> I went with Adrian Cronin: he was head of the department by then, and I was doing the commentary. Unfortunately, for the week that I was there I still had to do *The Gay Byrne Show* every morning. We were in Radio Luxembourg, in a foreign station with foreign people. It just made the show a little more difficult than normal to do. All the while we were attending all the ESC press conferences and so on, and I was up beside Terry Wogan. I had listened to Radio Luxembourg all of my young life, and I suddenly found myself in the studios where Pete Murray and Peter Madren operated 208, Radio Luxembourg. It was actually just a relatively small house, with nice radio studios. It was a hard week's work. All the other commentators were free to loll around the place and attend an odd press conference here and there; we were working all day. John Caden was my producer and we had to work all day getting the next day's radio programme done.

Then, on the Saturday night after we were finished, we were on the first flight out on Sunday. We had a radio show to do all the following week. It wasn't exactly a holiday for me, and I decided, I don't want to do this any more.

Paul Lyttle was one of the backing singers in Luxembourg:

Linda was still the singer in my band when she went to Luxembourg, but she and I had parted ways. I was one of her backing singers, and I was there with them the night that the song was recorded with Bill Whelan, who did the arrangement. I paid for the recording and was still very much involved. That was one of the most exciting nights. I sang backing vocals on the night, along with Alan Pentony (the band's bass player) and Pat Reilly (who sang backing vocals in RTÉ for about fifteen years on Eurovision). That was a great week. Terry Wogan gave us a push with promoting it. He did something unbelievable: he came and met us one day, and allowed us to have a photoshoot with Linda. We'd great publicity in all the papers. In those days the Eurovision was so important. One single would sell millions of records, so it was worth signing the act even for just that one record, and that's something that can't be said now. Portugal gave us no points on the last vote, and we only needed two to guarantee a win.

Linda remembers the voting only too well:

I remember that the auditorium was small compared to anything these days. The first vote came through and it was twelve points for Ireland. That was a shock for me. Then I remembered about horses and races, and how the horse in the lead rarely wins. We were in the lead and people were congratulating us. I was sitting there as green as the grass, to be honest with you. Then Portugal, the very last vote, didn't vote for Ireland, and we lost. It was unbelievable. A cousin of mine was working in a very posh hotel in London at that stage, and there was a group of Portuguese people who had come in with a lot of luggage, and he told them to hump it up to the room themselves.

I did feel that I had the better song. When we went to the reception afterwards, there were commiserations and congratulations. I know that we didn't win, but it certainly did me no harm. That was the start of working in Europe, and it was just the start of my association with the Eurovision that is still there today. I do remember that there was a contract on the cards with Sony Records, and there was a vast amount of money riding on the win. Even though I lost all of the money and didn't win, doors in Europe opened at the same time. That was when I was able to start working outside of Ireland. You lose financially but you gain in other ways.

Someone who did lose financially that night was Shay Healy:

I negotiated Linda Martin's contract in 1984 with 'Terminal 3', and we were beaten on the very last vote. We lost to The Herreys, and the next morning I remember being outside a coffee shop and feeling devastated. When I got home, I heard the story of the two top executives at CBS, who had taxied a private jet onto the runway at Heathrow Airport, ready to take off, and arrive in Luxembourg in time for the craic. But the minute Linda lost, they turned the plane around and taxied back in, and the two executives went home. I met one of them a few years later, Tony Woolcott, and I asked him if the story was true. He said, 'I'm afraid it is.'

The following year, Maxi was writing and creating even more records:

By 1985 I had started to write rather than sing. Patricia O'Brien sang 'Hold Her Now' for me. Patricia is the daughter of Brendan O'Brien of the Dixies, and Trish had been doing some backing vocals. I loved her voice. I also had two songs that year. The second song was the surplus song. Jacinta White, whom I had worked with in theatre and who has gone on to have a great UK career in music, sang it. I got the idea from Marion of Fossett's Circus, who had gone back to the circus at the time that Denis and I wrote 'Circus Song'. I had two songs in the National Song Contest. That's another record.

Marion Fossett was later back as a soloist with 'Only a Fantasy'. Mike Sherrard would sing 'Hearts', written by his brother. Johnny Logan remembers this one:

That was a folk song. I was working in a studio in London, and I did that song and really liked it. I was doing demos at that point, and it got into the National Song Contest. My brother is a great singer. I think Mick is more of a rock singer. I don't think the format of the National Song Contest ever suited him, and he sang it for me, but unfortunately it was one of those songs that should have been five minutes long, and it didn't really work condensing it into three minutes for the Eurovision. It's a great song, but it didn't really work over three minutes.

All of these entries would play second fiddle to 'Wait until the Weekend Comes', another composition by the brilliant Brendan Graham. Maria McCabe was born in Dublin, but grew up in Dundalk with her four siblings. She got into music at the age of five, when she won a pub singing competition, and continued to be successful across County Louth. She was ninety-five percent blind from the age of nine, but continued to sing. Her Dad suggested the surname 'Christian', as it suited every language. Brendan recalls when he first heard her voice:

One of the things that you develop over the years is an ear for beautiful, extraordinary voices. I heard Maria Christian on demos up in Slane, in a studio of John Donoghue – 'John D'. When the song was done, I thought she'd be great. That's how Maria came to do it. She was from Dundalk, and she was fantastic – an absolute gem to work with. She had a great voice.

What's Another Year?

Maria remembers her NSC experience:

> Flo McSweeney did the original demo of 'Wait Until The Weekend Comes', and she got picked to do the National Song Contest. But Brendan heard about me and asked me to come to Dublin to sing the song. When he heard me singing the song, he said: 'You're gonna win the National.' He obviously liked the way I was putting it across. It's a nice song. Flo was upset. The year before, Brendan had gone to Chile with her. I think the song finished third. So he picked me to do the National Song Contest. I was an outsider and an unknown singer. There was a well-known singer there, Jacinta Whyte, who was linked to somebody important in Dublin. I think she was the favourite, and the one they expected to win. It was in the pocket, and that's it. At the rehearsals, they didn't like my outfit, they didn't like my hair and they didn't like my make-up.
>
> I remember that I had one flower, a wee orchid that Brendan had got me, in the dressing room. Everyone else had tonnes of flowers and cards. I looked at that wee flower and said, 'Me and you are going to get out there tonight and we are going to do it'. I was only nineteen, and I sang my heart out. It was the performance that did it, I think. A bit like Dana's. It was just like a dream. I remember waking up the next day and I felt like a princess. There's a scene in *Gone With the Wind* where Scarlett O Hara wakes up in the bed one morning, and she's stretching, and everything seems so perfect in life. Well, that's how I felt. It was lovely. People would ask me for my autograph when I walked down the street. It was a great experience. You feel like a star. I did *The Late Late Show* with Gay Byrne. Gay was such an icon. My mam and dad came to see it. It was an unbelievable gift for them.

In Gothenburg, Brendan would be in competition with a man with whom he would later successfully co-write, but for now his main concern was for Ireland to do well. That, and running around Gothenburg Harbour in his green tracksuit. He remembers Sweden:

We came sixth. I remember Bobbysocks won with a Rolf Lovland song. The thing that I remember about Gothenburg was the fantastic Noel Kelehan. There was an upstairs bar in the hotel where we stayed, with a piano in it. We were all there, right up at the top. Noel got on the piano and, in his completely unique way, played a version of 'Danny Boy' with Mary [Brendan's wife] singing it. It was slightly jazz infused, but it was magical and everyone loved it. Noel just sat there with the cigarette hanging out of his mouth. We could have been in a speakeasy in Chicago, and I remember that, and it was just a great experience to see this marvellous musician. We'd been used to seeing him out at the front, and here he was actually doing the business himself. That's really one of the strong memories I have of Gothenburg.

Marie, however, has mixed emotions about her time in Sweden:

I had none of my family with me, which was the only sad thing about it. My mam and dad would have been too poor at the time – he was just a plasterer. We would never have thought of asking RTÉ to bring them out. A lot of people came out with me, a lot of people that were unnecessary, and none of them took care of me. One of those people should have been my mum. Because you're so young, you just think how great it is that you're there. You don't ask any questions, you just obey. As I got older and had kids of my own, I re-alised that, if my twenty-one-year-old daughter was repre-senting Ireland, I'd have made sure that I was with her. I think my parents would have been a bit too ignorant and too afraid to say it. I think it was a disgrace that I was sent over there without one family member. The plane was packed. I didn't know who they were, but there were tonnes of people on that plane. It was full of my entourage, but I didn't know anyone except Noel Kelehan and the backing singers.

If nobody took care of Maria while she was there, one person, a former Eurovision winner, certainly noticed her throughout the week. Maria explains:

When I went over to Sweden nobody knew that I was blind. I didn't talk about my blindness because I was young and I didn't want people thinking I was blind. As Ireland were first on that year, I opened the competition. The Herreys had opened the competition the year before, so Richard came up to me while I was there in my evening dress and said, 'I just want to wish you luck. You're going to be on first tonight, and it brought us good luck last year because we won.' I thanked him, pretending I could see. When I went back over to the group, they said to me that it had been Richard Herrey, one of the winners from last year. The girls were saying, 'Oh he's gorgeous.' Then the show happened and I did well, I came sixth. At the end of the evening there was a big ball with an orchestra. I arrived with Noel Kelehan and the backing singers. There were all these photographers and flashing lights when I arrived, like how you see in Hollywood, but I couldn't see. Then Richard Herrey, who had waited for me at the door, took me by the hand and said, 'Can I escort you to your table?' It was lovely. Then that was it, he fell for me. Richard Herrey fell in love with me. I came home the next day, and he flew to Ireland a few days later and said that he wanted to marry me.

Maria didn't marry Richard. She moved to France in the '90s and is now married with seven children. In 2016 she appeared on the Irish TV show *The Voice*, and is now pursuing her music career again.

Brendan was back in the final in 1986 with 'Here in the Night', sung by Fran Meen. Honor Heffernan and Cork band Loudest Whisper were also there, as was John Spillane, duetting with Mandy Murphy on 'Ringo.' According to John:

It was based on a cowboy called Johnny Ringo from the movies. I used to pretend I was him when we played cowboys and Indians long ago. I'd say possibly Ringo Starr might have got his name from him as well? And Johnny Ringo MacDonogh?

Johnny Logan's brother Mike was also there, with 'If I Could Change Your Mind', as Johnny recalls:

> That's a great song. That's one that I wrote in London. It's a five-minute song that was written very much along the lines of Jacques Brel, written at the piano. I thought that it was one of the best songs I wrote from that period, because it was a very honest song. I also thought it touched on a very adult theme. Musically and lyrically it married very beautifully.

Maxi's songwriting continued to bear fruit, as she'd written another song for the final:

> Theresa Lowe sang a song I co-wrote called 'Only the Lonely Survive'. I started to compère [laughs] the National Song Contest with Marty Whelan, when Johnny won in 1987 in the Gaiety. I compèred it and then went into compèring it on radio for the Eurovision, so I've been there in every single capacity. Singer-songwriter, writer not singer, singer with Maxi, Dick and Twink, singer solo, singer with Sheeba, and then compering it, and compering the Eurovision on radio. Not only am I a fan of the Eurovision, I've been indelibly imprinted on it.

All these couldn't hold a candle to Newry band Luv Bug. Formed in 1977, the band included family members Max, Hugh and lead singer June Cunningham, with Ricky Meyler and Majella Grant. Their debut single, 'Red Light Spells Danger', charted in 1984, and they'd been touring the country continuously, including the Tullamore Harriers, where I'd seen them on many occasions and had become a huge fan. Their live shows consisted of a mix of current chart hits and their own original material. By the time of the NSC they'd had several top-thirty hits in Ireland, including the fantastic 'On My Own'. Max explains how they got involved:

Our manager Mickey Magill was told about a song that Athlone songwriter Kevin Sheerin had written. Kevin sent a demo of it to my house in Newry. We listened to it and thought, we can do something with this great song. So we got together and came up with a version of it that we thought would suit. The rest is history. We entered the contest with a positive attitude but could only dream of winning. It was certainly an unbelievable night for us. Looking back on it, it was even bigger than we imagined at the time.

This year was the twenty-first anniversary of the NSC, and June remembers it vividly:

Mike Murphy hosted the show that night. I remember after we won they brought out a cake to celebrate the anniversary. We were presented with a medal to commemorate that. It was absolutely amazing, for us and for all the folks back home in Newry who were watching.

Luv Bug were everywhere after that, with television appearances and radio interviews. At the same time, they were gigging constantly. They even got the front cover of the *RTÉ Guide*. The song reached number two in the charts; ironically, it was kept off the spot by another song of the same name. June remembers how Norway's second city, Bergen, was the location for the thirty-first Eurovision:

Bergen and its people were amazing. They showed us all around the city, treating us like royalty. When we were returning home, they presented us with a detailed architect's drawing of Bergen. We were delighted with fourth; we got three twelve-point scores from Austria, Spain and Denmark. We're just very fortunate to have had that experience. Needless to say it also did no harm to our musical career.

The publicity from the Eurovision enabled Luv Bug, in collaboration with RTÉ, to release their debut album in 1987. Luv Bug were scouted by legendary producer Roy Thomas Baker (known for Queen, The Cars, T'Pau and so on), who brought them to Los Angeles to work on material. They subsequently signed to Richard Branson's 'Virgin Records' as Heart of Ice. Thirty-seven years after forming, Luv Bug decided to take a break from performing.

By 1987, a lot of acts were making their debut in the NSC; the late Spyder Simpson and Paul Duffy, to name two. An Irish-language song would also make the final for the first time in five years, when Valerie Armstrong sang '*Ó D'imigh Tú Uaim*'. Making a return to the final were Loudest Whisper and Charlie McGettigan. Charlie explains his return:

> I always write just for the sake of writing songs. If I thought I had something that was good enough to represent the country rather than win, or something that we could be proud of, that's what you were about. We wrote a song for Ireland that we wouldn't be apologising for, and continue to write, though not necessarily songs for the Eurovision. 'Hold Me Now' was a great song. It's a perfect example of a great, great song. Johnny knows how to put a song together, he just knows the right way to put the words together.

Once again, Charlie found himself up against a song written by Johnny Logan. Johnny explains how he ended up back in the final:

> I was living in a house with five students in Wandsworth Common when 'Hold Me Now' was written. It was 1985. The record company were giving me songs and they were all shite, so I decided I would try and write one for myself. The first attempt was called 'Me and My Jealous Heart', which I gave to my brother. It came third in the Castlebar Song Contest. The second song I wrote was 'Hold Me Now'. I demoed it with the producer I was working with, in one take on the piano. It was about five and a half minutes long, and I kept it for two years. Then Louis called me and

Rowland Soper and Dickie Rock jet off to Luxembourg in 1966
(Rowland Soper Collection)

Muriel Day: Ireland's first female representative in 1969
(Malcolm McDowell/Muriel Day Collection)

Maxi and Cliff Richard in Luxembourg in 1973
(Daniel De Chenu/Maxi Collection)

Stacc, finalists in the 1978 N.S.C. (left to right) Catriona Walsh, Des Moore, Bill Whelan,
John Drummand, Nicola Kerr and Desi Reynolds
(Bill Whelan Collection)

Happy Men: Cathal Dunne and his father, Gerard celebrate winning the N.S.C in 1979
(Cathal Dunne Collection)

Shay Healy, Johnny Logan and Tom McGrath celebrate their win at the Hague
(Shay Healy Collection)

A Sort of Homecoming: Shay Healy celebrates with his sons and father at Dublin Airport
(Shay Healy Collection)

Sheeba's Eurovision promotional photoshoot in 1981
(Maxi Collection)

Luv Bug's Max Cunningham's National Song Contest wnners medal from 1986
(Luv Bug Collection)

Majella Grant and Jane Cunningham of Luv Bug with Terry Wogan in Bergen
(Luv Bug Collection)

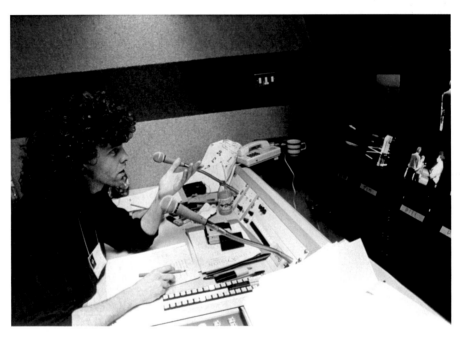

Declan Lowney becomes Eurovision's youngest producer in 1988
(Declan Lowney Collection)

Swede Dreams: Linda Martin and Johnny Logan celebrate their victory in 1992
(Linda Martin Collection)

Mill-Treat: Brendan Balfe and Shay Healy help celebrate Niamh's winning moment in 1993
(Niamh Kavanagh Collection)

Rock 'n' Roll Kids: Charlie McGettigan, Paul Harrington and Brendan Graham toast their victory in 1994

Rolf Lovland and Fionnuala Sherry of Secret Garden with the author of this book
(Mick Lynch Collection)

Winning Voice: Noel Kelehan, Eimear Quinn and Brendan Graham celebrate with the rest of the Irish musicians in 1996
(Brendan Graham Collection)

Marc Roberts performs 'Mysterious Woman' at the E.S.C Final in 1997
(Marc Roberts Collection)

Eamon Toal and Larry Gogan celebrate the new Millennium in Stockholm
(Eamon Toal Collection)

Jedward and Leanne Moore performed at consecutive Eurovisions in 2011 and 2012
(Leanne Moore Collection)

The Winners Take It All: The Irish Eurovision Winners Tour in 2012
(Mick Lynch Collection)

Friends For Nearly 40 Years: Shay Healy and Johnny Logan in 2012
(Pete Brennan Collection)

Leanne Moore and Graham Norton at the 2013 Eurovision Song Contest
(Leanne Moore Collection)

Marty Whelan, Conor Mulhall and Ryan Dolan at the ESC in Malmo in 2013
(Conor Mulhall Collection)

Rock 'n' Roll Kids 20th Anniversary: Shay, Pete Brennan, Charlie, Paul and Brendan
(Mick Lynch Collection)

Phil Coulter, robbed of a second Eurovision win, with the author
(Mick Lynch Collection)

Brendan Graham, writer of four Eurovision entries, with the next generation of Eurovision fans, Anna and Mikey Lynch at the National Concert Hall (Mick Lynch Collection)

Eurovision's most distinguished conductor, the late Noel Kelehan (Mary Kelehan Collection)

asked me to put a song into the National Song Contest. He liked this song, and it ran away with it.

At Johnny's second Eurovision in Brussels, he was better prepared for what was ahead. The omens looked good:

> I knew, and those around me knew, that we had a really good chance in Brussels. Every time I rehearsed it, all the cleaning ladies came into the auditorium and applauded. Every time I sang it, the orchestra applauded. That was kind of a surprise. I was one of the favourites. The song was really strong, as was the performance and the way I looked. '*Gente Di Mare*' was the only song I was worried about, and I'm great friends with Umberto Tozzi. We performed '*Gente Di Mare*' together in front of 22,000 people. I probably learnt too much from my experience in 1980. I knew exactly what I was doing in 1987. In 1980 it was all very innocent; in '87 I felt the pressure of being a winner. I sometimes think that the hardest person to beat in your second Eurovision is yourself. I had to overcome the fear.

He certainly did overcome the fear, and gave a brilliant performance. He was clearly emotional when he was unable to complete the last note, but kept his composure enough to once again say that he 'still loves Ireland'. The Eurovision was on its way back to the Emerald Isle.

CHAPTER FIVE
EURO '88

Dublin celebrated its Millennium in 1988, so it was no surprise that the capital was picked to host the thirty-third Eurovision. Just as in 1981, the RDS Simmonscourt would be the venue. Brendan Graham was back in the National Final with another song, 'Lifeline'. It was sung by Bagatelle's front man, Liam Reilly. Liam recalls:

> I had a number one with 'Summer in Dublin' in 1980, then a number one with 'Streets of New York', and had a few more, including Paddy Reilly with 'The Flight of Earls'. I did not consider the Eurovision much until 1988, when Brendan Graham asked me to sing his song, and I said I'm not going to do it on piano for a change. The lovely Angelina Ball was singing it with me. I was just a gobshite wearing a striped jacket; I was out of my depth, with no piano in front of me. I know the guys from Jump The Gun won it. We came second, but I wasn't going to go and shoot myself over it; it was just a bit of fun.

While Brendan Graham would finish runner-up this time, he would finally redeem himself with the locals in County Mayo when Linda Martin sang his song 'If I Should Ever Lose Your Love', which won the last Castlebar Song Contest. Louis Walsh's Jump The Gun would represent Ireland on home territory, and Wexford's Declan Lowney became the youngest director of the Eurovision Song Contest. Before the event even took place, Declan found himself in hot water.

Declan Lynch interviewed me for the *Sunday Independent*. Unusually, it wouldn't happen now, we just sat in the canteen. Nobody came with me, it was just me and him chatting. He recorded the chat. My view of the Eurovision was that it was a bit of a dinosaur, something I had worked very hard to change. Ultimately, I felt, it was an excuse for a bunch of TV executives to go on the piss for a week. I got a bit personal as I talked about the British entry, Scott Fitzgerald. I remember he had this ridiculous suit with these huge lapels, and the Swedes sent a girl who was six months pregnant who couldn't do her dance routine. I said some sadly inappropriate things, and Declan Lynch ran the piece and milked it.

I swore a few times and RTÉ were outraged, and rightly so. There were calls the next morning for me to be taken off the show. I remember going into the canteen the Monday morning and someone had taken the article, enlarged it and put it on the notice board. It was all over the fucking place. Certain people on the show said they didn't want to work with me because they felt I'd let them down. The head of entertainment wanted to bring in a new director, but Liam [Miller] was very good. He stood with me and made me go around to every department head that I'd mentioned and apologise and explain myself. At the end of the day what I'd said was immature but it had no reflection on all the great work we were doing and we were going to put on a great show, and really it was a very humbling experience for me, and a lovely thing for him to do, to stick by me.

Celine Dion, an unknown Canadian representing Switzerland and singing in French, had lost her luggage during the week. She would win the contest by the narrowest of margins. All this was happened long before she sang the theme from '*Titanic*'. Fionnuala Sherry was part of the RTÉ Orchestra that year, for her first Eurovision, and she remembers Celine's win:

I don't think her win took everyone by surprise, but I was so caught up in the orchestral end of things that I wasn't focused on the actual singers. I just remember her at the very start being a very quiet individual. I don't think any of us saw what she would blossom into, how she would become the amazing world star that she now is.

Kiev Connolly's eighteenth place finish in Lausanne in 1989 would be our worst placing to date, but as we moved into a new decade, Irish songwriters were concentrating more on writing World Cup songs than Eurovision ones. At one stage the top five spots in the Irish charts were dominated by them. The Memories (who would go on to have a number one with 'The Game', a parody of Billy Joel's 'We Didn't Start the Fire' later that year) were in the national final with 'If It Means Losing You'. Linda Martin was back again, this time with friends. Liam Reilly returned with his own song 'Somewhere in Europe'. He recalls how the song came to be entered:

> I had met a girl from Germany in the States. When I was back and in my friend Tommy Mangan's house (a great friend of mine for many years, and a great keyboard player), I played him this song I'd written, 'Somewhere in Europe'. He said I should record it. He brought out this reel-to-reel tape recorder and put it on top of the piano. He recorded the song and sent it in to RTÉ. I was back in Philadelphia when I got a call from one of the researchers to say that I was in the National Song Contest final, and that I I had to come home the next day and register. I wrote it in 1990 in about an hour. It was just 'Meet me in Paris . . . ' and all those places. I do it on stage now every night. Thank God we don't have to write it now, or there would be twenty-seven verses.

The final that year was held in the Gaiety Theatre and presented by Jimmy Greeley and Clíona Ní Bhuachalla. Liam recalls a funny moment:

> The best laugh about it was that The Memories were there, and one of the lads in the band said to me there was a line

in 'Somewhere In Europe' that said 'The memories refuse to go away' and they just laughed and if you ever look at the clip of me singing the song, when I'm singing that line I just burst into a smile and I nearly laughed and messed the whole thing up. You would not believe the camaraderie in the green room that night. It's a tough business and one night in the spotlight doesn't make up for all the tough nights. It was a great experience to win the bloody thing and to go to Yugoslavia.

Liam did eventually get to Yugoslavia, after a delayed flight and getting lost somewhere in Europe and missing rehearsals.

It was very last minute. I was with Adrian Cronin, who is since deceased, and some women from RTÉ. A lot of work went into it, and Noel Kelehan had the orchestra at the top of their game. We had five days of rehearsal. In the supermarkets in Zagreb there might be soap on the shelves one day and bread the next. It was the beginning of the war, and the Croatians were driving around with Croatian flags. Every night when I performed the song, Ken, the bass player, always said, 'This is a song that represented Ireland in Yugoslavia for Radovan Karadzic and Slobodan Milosevic.' It just goes to show you what can come of singing the wrong song in the wrong place. My parents were staying in Dubrovnik and my brothers and sisters were in Split. They were coming up to Zagreb because you couldn't get a room in Zagreb. The only decent hotel in Zagreb was the one where all the contestants were staying. You could go to a delegation's party every night and you got to meet lots of people. I met and still know Sarah Bray (who represented Luxembourg). I still keep in touch with the Portuguese contestant. She's still entertaining in Portugal.

Liam remembers got a call from an newspaper on the morning of the contest:

This guy from the *Sunday World* newspaper rang me in my hotel room in Zagreb on the morning of the song contest

and said, 'We just want to know what you had for breakfast.'
I said, 'Listen, thanks for the call but I can't believe you
asked me what I had for breakfast.' These are the funny
things you remember.

That evening before the contest, Liam was once again dealing with the media:

> I had a very emotional moment when Jimmy Greeley asked
> me to come up to the commentary box. I went up and I
> looked out and saw my mum and dad and sisters all there
> with these wee Irish flags. That was very emotional. I asked
> Collette (the head of the delegation) to tell me something
> that would keep my confidence up, and she said, 'There's
> only five hundred million people watching.' Then she said,
> 'Well there's only one or two thousand people in the
> stadium.' I felt OK because I've played to that number of
> people in the RDS and the Opera House. I said to myself,
> 'Right here I go. I'll do my best and be nice.' I had two
> backing singers, Mary Downes and Kim Jackson.

While Liam's performance would go off without a hitch, Spain weren't so lucky,
and had technical issues. Liam felt sorry for them, but there was something else he
wasn't impressed with:

> I was well ahead, watching in the green room with Mary and
> Kim. When Italy voted the presenters spoke in Italian, and
> you're supposed to use either English or French. As far as
> I could understand it they were stalling for time. The nail
> in the coffin was when Ireland gave Italy the twelve points.
> I don't understand the psychology behind it and there is no
> bitterness, but maybe they couldn't afford to stage it [laughs
> out loud]. The people in RTÉ said to me, 'You could go the
> whole way with this.' My record company executive Paul
> Keogh was there and I was guaranteed a certain amount
> from the record company if I won it, but that went out the
> window after the Irish vote. It was a lot of money down the
> drain, but the song was still released in ten or twelve coun-

tries, and I'm still getting royalties. I'm a very shy person, but I went over to Toto's table to congratulate him. He just nodded. When he went up to receive his prize, his Grecian 2000 was already running down his white jacket. He had to take the jacket off. I like his song, it was very topical. I always laugh about how the guy that beat me is called Toto Cutogno. I haven't heard of him since. After I got home I remember watching the Italia '90 world cup with my cousin in Glasnevin. When I saw the Irish team's green jerseys I said to my cousin, 'Jaysus it must be great to represent your country like that.' He turned to me and said, 'Are you alright in the head? You just did.' The bastard that put us out was called Toto Schillaci, and I said, 'If I meet another guy called Toto, I'll kill him.'

The following year Liam was back in the national final, but this time Kim was the vocalist. She beat Johnny Logan's brother Mike Sherrard. Liam was making history as the first songwriter to write consecutive Irish entries for the Eurovision. He explains how he came to write a song for Kim:

Kim Jackson ended up singing with my own band who were on the road after the Eurovision. Kim was doing backing vocals, and I told her I'd write a song for her and put it into the National Song Contest. I told her, 'You're better looking than me, and I'm not doing it again.' We won it and went out to Rome. The great thing about Rome was that I didn't have to rehearse every day. I walked around the Trevi Fountain and went to see the Colosseum. It is very different going there as a performer as opposed to just being the songwriter. In 1990 when I was both performer and songwriter I had to talk to everyone – songwriters, performers and publishers.

Liam remembers a funny incident:

Myself and Terry Wogan couldn't get into the big old cinema complex. We were wearing badges with composer and commentator written on them, and still couldn't get in. Terry turned around and sayid, 'Well Reilly, what'll we do?' I said, 'Sure, two Irishmen outside the door in Rome, we'll wait till someone's looking for us.' I actually heard the song when I was in the corridor beside the stage. My sisters and my two brothers-in-law were there. I was busy greeting people I'd met at previous contests. Sarah Bray, who was back working in the bank in Luxembourg, said, 'I can't believe you won the Irish contest twice.' I haven't seen her now for many years. I asked Kim to go for the top note and she said, 'I don't know if I can reach it.' I said, 'Of course you can. Go for it, it's yours.'

In Italy, Kim was backed by Jenny Newman, Miriam Courtney and Denis Doran. She would finish a respectable tenth. Kim stayed in the music business and today runs her own successful music school. Summing up her Eurovision experience in Rome, she said:

I came, I saw, I didn't conquer, I went home!

In 1992 Linda Martin gave it yet another shot, with another Johnny Logan song. Linda recalls:

I remember Louis ringing and saying: 'Johnny has another song for you.' He doesn't live that far from me, and I went out to him. It was just Johnny singing with the piano. He said, 'I'm going to put it in, and if it gets through, it's yours.' It was a very rough version of 'Why Me' that got through. There was a middle-eight, if I remember rightly. The bridge wasn't there when the demo was put in. We went across to Frank McNamara's studio, and he started working on it. Most of it was done, but we were still missing a middle-eight. I remember coming home and being in bed asleep when the phone rang. It was Johnny: 'I've got the middle-eight, get out of your bed, get back over here.' I got back up, and went straight back over to Frank McNamara's. He had the middle-eight written, and we knew we had something special.

107

Johnny remembers the inspiration for the song:

> I'd written 'Why Me' for my wife about two years earlier,
> and demoed it over in Frank McNamara's studio in
> Dunshaughlin and in Ashbourne. I was sitting in my music
> room looking out at my wife in the garden, and wondering
> how anyone could live with a working musician for so long.
> We'd been married for fourteen years that year. The song
> was written in about forty-tive minutes. Louis called and
> asked if I could prepare a song for Linda for the National
> Song Contest, and I had 'Why Me'. I tried to sit down and
> write a song to win the contest for Linda, but everything I
> tried to write sounded very contrived while 'Why Me' was
> from my heart. So I adapted 'Why Me' and changed one of
> the lines so Linda could sing it. Then I edited the song down
> from four minutes to three. The rest is history.

Linda comfortably beat Patricia Roe and The Last Word to win the NSC, but before she left for Sweden her dress had to be chosen. Paul Moreland (who designed hats) rang Louis Walsh, then spoke to Kevin Lenihan and sent in a dress design in white. The colour didn't work well on camera in an empty RTÉ studio, so they ended up with grey. Some people think it's green, but grey was what worked best on camera. With the dress sorted, Linda headed to Malmö, this time better prepared because she had done it all before. She explains:

> I knew more of what to do. The second time around I knew
> there was a lot of propaganda in it. It was time to court the
> press in all the different countries. I remember Malmö being
> very cold and very quiet, but full of incredibly kind people.
> I have always liked Swedish people. I worked the Saturday
> night before our flight as we hadn't a shilling in our pockets.
> We were normal musicians earning our crust on the road.
> We left Dublin very early on the Sunday morning, and our
> rehearsals were on Monday and Wednesday. It was a twenty
> minute rehearsal, and the clock started even if you hadn't
> arrived. If you were late, tough shit! When they started to
> do the camera shots, Kevin Lenihan, who was our

delegation leader, *plámásed* the producer, shall we say, with Irish whiskey and a large lunch. He suggested that we have eight camera shots, because we didn't want something that was run of the mill. Kevin is an absolute gentleman and he did it the right way, and we got the shots we wanted. On Friday afternoon everyone was back in for a dress rehearsal. That night there was another dress rehearsal, and then a very, very important one on Saturday afternoon. That dress rehearsal was streamed to the jury, ensuring that if there were any problems in transmission on the night, at least the jury would have all twenty-five songs. They would be able to listen and debate and cast their votes so there was no time wasted when the actual contest came around which is just before the public viewing. The contest was that night, and the Irish delegation was going mental. I remember that the orchestra started and then away we went. We couldn't have done any more. That was my gut feeling, afterwards. We did everything we could. We had backing vocalists who went from bass up to high soprano, we covered every single note you could cover and everything else in between. The costumes were perfect, the orchestra was perfect and that was it.

The competition was tough, with three songs cited as favourites. Participating for the UK was Michael Ball, someone Linda got to know very well and is still a great friend of to this day. Mary Spiteri, representing Malta, was christened 'rising damp' by the Irish party. Linda remembers the voting;

We just sat back and waited. It didn't start off well when Spain gave us nothing, then it went to Turkey. I knew, since Johnny and myself had worked extensively in Turkey, that they would give us twelve points. They did, and so it went on and on. It ended up being between Michael and myself. I can't remember what country it was that didn't vote for Michael, but it was then that we knew. I remember knowing we couldn't be beaten. I think we were about three or four voters from the end, and that was it. You do have to try and have a bit of decorum and sit there and pretend 'Ah, sure I don't really care', but I think I nearly hit the ceiling. It was just amazing. I remember thinking *Thanks be to*

God, I can get off the road. Being on the road is fine, when you're young. When you start getting a bit older, especially if you're a woman, it's not a great situation to be in. I just remember thinking *Thank God for that.* I started doing corporate functions, and then most of my work was in Europe. It was just heaven

Johnny Logan created history with his third victory. He was there to celebrate:

I was happy for both of us when Linda won. To be honest, I was exhausted while I was there. There had been an air strike, and I had had to drive for about six hours the day before the contest to get to an airport outside of Germany so that I could actually get to Malmö. I arrived just in time for the contest, the day before. I was very confident that Linda was going to be in the top three, and I knew if we got the right run of the dice that it would win. I really felt strongly about the song. I told her, at the beginning, that if she worked with me on this, we had a really good chance of winning. That song was perfect for an orchestra.

After Linda won in Malmö, the presenter said to her, 'See you next year in Dublin'. How wrong he was. Cork man, Noel C. Duggan, had other ideas. He wrote to RTÉ and offered them the opportunity to host the event in little known Millstreet in County Cork. Though the Green Glens Arena was ordinarily used for indoor showjumping, RTÉ gave it the green light. Noel and the Duggan family asked Linda to open it. She was flown down by helicopter, and awaiting her was a saddled horse named Aaron. This was for the press to signify that Millstreet had got the deal for the Eurovision.

Niamh Kavanagh wouldn't have been a name familiar to the public at this time, but would have been well known in the industry, especially after singing on *The Commitments* Soundtrack. Niamh explains how she got involved in the NSC:

A friend of mine was involved in it prior to '93. Kim Jackson and I were great mates, and she was involved in the nationals in 1991. We got to know each other after that and became great friends, funnily enough, over the years previous to that I had occasionally been approached with songs, but I never really wanted to do them. I was doing a lot of good work at that time and I was still working during the day. I was doing a lot of studio work up in Dublin and I was gigging. I was working a lot as a singer, and I was really happy with my life and my work. The Eurovision wasn't very well regarded among musicians, so you would have been cagey about been involved. There was no song that really ignited me until Jimmy Walsh's 'In Your Eyes'. I had worked with Brendan Graham a couple of times. He's a good friend of Bill Whelan's. Bill said to him, 'Do you have that song?' and then Brendan said to Jimmy, 'You should get Niamh to sing the song.' Jimmy sent it to me and I really loved it. I remember saying to my mother, 'This is a great song, but I'm not sure I want to do Eurovision.' Kim said to me, 'What's the worst that can happen? You go on and do good TV and come off.' Kim was instrumental in encouraging me to go do it. Then Jimmy said, 'You can make this whatever you want it to be.' He was right. It was such a good song, so I kind of agreed over Christmas.

Brendan Graham remembers suggesting the song to Niamh:

I think I was the one who played 'In Your Eyes' to Niamh Kavanagh first. I thought Niamh would be right for it when I heard it. We were driving around Stephen's Green and I said, 'Have a listen to this.' I was delighted when she decided to do it. She was a powerhouse, she was just phenomenal.

This year all the songs were performed on the 'Kenny Live' show that went out on a Saturday night. The public got to hear one a week until all the songs were performed. Niamh remembers the crazy preparation:

The launch was early January, and the draw was done for the 'Kenny Live' programme. We were first out, which meant that we had from about the eight of January to the sixteenth of January to make a backing track, find backing singers and make that song what it was. We were very lucky to have Frank McNamara on board, he was amazing. At that stage most people had their backing singers. We were lucky that we got such a lovely group: Gareth, Martina and Trisha. We hit the stage a week and a half later, having been all over the place. It was slightly different to the actual Eurovision final version we did, because the hysterics weren't quite there. I did that in the studio and then that became the song.

The final that year wasn't held in RTÉ. The running order was the same as for the 'Kenny Live' appearance a few weeks earlier, so Niamh was the first to perform. She recalls:

That show was in The Point Depot. It was a big live show with an orchestra. I was first, followed by Suzanne Bushnell, Patricia Roe and so on. I seem to recall somebody saying to me: 'We've got a great placement, we're in the middle, something to remember.' I joked, 'Well you're right, but you all have to follow me.' We were having a ball and loving that we were on first, then we could relax and there was no pressure. The general feeling that year was that it was Patricia's [Roe] year, but it's open to everyone. I didn't expect to win the National, let alone the way we did and it was a bit of a shocker.

If Niamh was slightly shocked by her victory, it was nothing compared to her employers, who were oblivious to the fact that she was even participating in the final. Niamh remembers:

I was working in AIB. They knew that I sang – I couldn't hide it. There was one time I was working shifts in the operations department. It was coming up to February in '92, and I had a split week off where I was finishing on a Wednesday night and wouldn't be back in until the following

Wednesday. I flew to New York that Wednesday night to do the Grammys, and then flew back in time for a gig down the local. I was always working. So I went to my manager the week of the national final and said, 'I'm doing this thing on Sunday night, and I was wondering if I could have Monday off as I'm only working from 10 AM to 4 PM. He said, 'That's not a problem. You can have the Monday off.' He didn't think anything of it. Then obviously on Monday morning it was all over the papers that an AIB teller had won the NSC – I wasn't actually a teller, I was in operations. Apparently the chief executive and marketing department were wondering, why nobody had told them. It was so normal for me to be singing that it hadn't occurred to me that the bank would be interested in it. There was a lot of talk when I came back in on Tuesday that they had missed a big marketing opportunity. They had it well in place by the time of the Eurovision. I worked right up to two weeks before I went to the Eurovision. Although I was doing fourteen interviews a day, they did give me some time off. I was doing as many shifts as I could, and I tried to keep things as normal as possible. I thought I'd be coming back, and wasn't expecting to win the Eurovision.

The next step for Niamh was to record the song professionally, but none of the record companies were really interested. Niamh explains:

They told me that they would sign me if I won. I remember one head of a record company saying to me, 'If you win, we'll sign you.' In my head I'd then be stuck with a company that didn't really want me. On the other hand, they said, 'If you don't win, you'll have a thousand pounds in your pocket.' I told Brendan Graham, 'I just can't sign up to that, it's not what I want.' Myself, Brendan and Jimmy paid for it to be recorded. We went to Frank [McNamara] and recorded the vocal and finished the track, and Frank did an amazing job on it. At 2 AM in the morning I was doing my final vocals. I'll never forget how wrecked I was. The hysterics happened at about 2 AM between Sunday night and Monday morning. The next morning we drove to Donegal, and I went to video my postcard.

The next stop for Niamh was Millstreet:

> I'll never forget going down to make the preview video with
> Pat Cowap. The director of the NSC Finals was on it. We
> got into a car and we drove down to Millstreet, and spent a
> week laughing. We made that video on a packet of crisps,
> seriously. I remember being on Millstreet filming a section
> of it in the convent. We arrived there and there wasn't even
> a way of making a cup of tea. I still remember how long
> that day was, but we had a brilliant week. Everybody stayed
> in Killarney, then travelled to Millstreet by bus. If you ar-
> rived late for rehearsals, you missed your slot. We went to
> the Green Glens Arena at around 10 AM every morning.
> There was excursions, of course, covering the whole area
> there. With Cork and Kerry involved it was an enormous
> undertaking.

While Europe might have been surprised with the location, Niamh gave it her blessing:

> There was a lot of talk about the 'cowsheds' and so on, and
> we were aware of all that. To be fair, I think there was general
> surprise when it was first chosen. I remember going down
> the first time, and all the reporters being brought down for
> the day. I remember in March and at the beginning of April
> how they were getting the grounds ready because they had to
> drop the whole floor. I was driving a digger. When you're a
> Eurovision entrant – or even a winner – you end up doing
> things you should never be let do. We went down and they
> gave us a tour of Millstreet, and you know how big Millstreet
> is, and we toured around it for about fifteen minutes. It was
> phenomenal what was being done and fantastic for the area.
> I think it was a really savvy move, because there was nothing
> else happening. If it had been in Dublin or any bigger city it
> would have been absorbed.

Linda was having trouble getting tickets for the Eurovision:

> I remember that year I was able to bring most of my family,

but I was only given two tickets by RTÉ. The National Lottery asked me to do a launch for it, and I said: 'I'll do it if you give me tickets.' So they gave me tickets, then Noel Duggan himself gave me a few more tickets, and my whole family came down and stayed in Killarney and enjoyed a Eurovision to top all Eurovisions. They had the most amazing time. It really was a fabulous production.

Linda wasn't the only one having problems with tickets that year. Niamh continues:

Tickets were gold dust. Jimmy [Walsh] and I were offered a ticket each for the Eurovision final. That's all we were allowed, so my mum decided she was going to rent a house near Millstreet. She drove down not knowing what it was going to be like. This is before you could look for a place on the Internet. She ended up in Noel C. Duggan's house having tea, and he rang around and organised a house for her in Banteer. A lot of my friends and family came down, (and there had been marquees set up outside the Green Glens Arena). My mum and dad did took two tickets for the dress rehearsal in the afternoon, that Pat Kenny had given them, I think. I gave my ticket to Jimmy so that he could have his parents there on the night. My mum and dad and all the family were in the white tent outside. That was the only way we could do it. When I did it in Norway in 2010, there were twenty thousand people in the audience. In Millstreet there were about three thousand. The National Lottery was sponsoring it, and there was one ticket per person. The family even had a better time than me because they were able to have a party in the tent.

Being one of the favourites didn't bother Niamh:

We were high on the ratings, but countries didn't tend to win two years in a row. I actually couldn't lose – all I had to do was sing well on the night and then it wouldn't matter if we won or lost because we'd won the year before. I was in one of the best positions ever, of, 'Sure it'll be grand.' There was no pressure on me in that regard. Even though people felt I should win, they didn't expect it to happen. I think Israel had been the last country to do it, in the late seventies. I remember 'Hallelujah' and 'I Wanna Be a Polar Bear'. I remember it being an exceptional achievement and that it rarely happened. We were considered popular, but it's hard to tell. Once you get into the Eurovision bubble everyone is a winner and you lose the ability to be objective.

Niamh wasn't the only one working in Millstreet. Tommy Nolan was part of the RTÉ stage crew, and remembers Millstreet fondly:

I was with them there in 1993. We were staying in a village in Killarney, and we'd drive over to Millstreet. It was all a front not wanting to win it. If you didn't want to win something, why would you enter it? In later years they sent Dustin out. They made a film about Millstreet called *Why Not Millstreet?* There was a guy at the end of it playing a harmonica playing the Eurovision anthem – that's me. We'd have our lunch and then go, 'Hi-ho, hi-ho, it's back to work we go.' Noel C. Duggan took this up. He loved it. He treated us very well, and I got to fly in a helicopter for the first time.

As 8 PM approached, Europe was watching, but Niamh wasn't worried:

I had a bit of a cold as I was working so hard all the way up to it. We did three dress rehearsals and it's a pretty busy week. It was so hot during the final week and then so cold that, by the time I got to the final, I just hoped that I could sing. So many people had sent me beautiful flowers – I used to have to take them out of my hotel room and put them in the bath so that I could sleep. There were a lot of lilies in particular. They're so heavily scented and so full of pollen that I couldn't even have them in the bathroom.I wasn't particularly nervous, as I knew I was on to a winner. All I needed was to sing well because it's very structured. I'd done the show three times in practice. I'm a bit odd in that I get nervous after an event;

I think it's the adrenaline rush. I get very nervous afterwards, but not very much before. I was relaxed about it all, the make-up and the hair, right up to the last minute standing at the side of the stage waiting. Eloise [the Swedish entry] were singing and I was waiting to go on and people in the stands spotted me. When they announced: 'Next is Ireland'. The place went mental. I was standing on stage and all I could see was Tom, the floor manager. I knew that the orchestra were behind me, and all the guys were there.

Playing in the orchestra that night, Fionnuala Sherry said:

I first met Rolf [Lovland] at Millstreet. He was conducting for the Norwegian entry, and conducted that song ['*Alle Mine Tankar*']. The 1993 Eurovision in Millstreet was a blast. It was so brave to do it down there. If the Irish want to do something, we do it well. They were so welcoming, and there was a great sense of wanting to be a part of it. It was a great week for us as musicians. It's not hard to play and socialise, and it's such an international cross-section of artists. Every country brings their own conductor, so you're working with a different conductor for every song. We had Noel Kelehan, who I adored. We were all very broke then and this was sort of a big bang of life in a boring and mundane time. When Millstreet came along we were all a little bit more confident, like, yeah, we can do this, yeah it was really special. It was a very happy time.

For Niamh, it was over before it began:

The music started, and next thing I knew I was done. I go off to the side, feeling composed and fabulous in my lovely Richard Lewis outfit, then I fell into a hole on the other side. I couldn't see it with all the lights, and I came off like a muppet. Then there was a round of applause and a standing ovation in the green room. Everyone got a round of applause when they came backstage. Security was so tight that during the show. At one point I went to the toilet, which was outside the green room, and wasn't let back in until I put my laminated pass back on. The minute the show was over though, they let anybody in to say hello. We went back into the green room, and the champagne started flowing. I'm not a drinker, and neither was John, the head of our delegation and nor were the backing singers. We all just sat there, getting on with things and chatting away while the voting was going on. It was outrageous and stressful. The first one was a 'twelve', the next was a 'one' but we did get votes from everybody. I don't think we missed a vote from anyone, which is unusual. There was the fault at the end when Malta hadn't voted, which was mental, and then there was the final win. At that point, about three or four voters from the end, I started to hyperventilate. I was thinking, *This is ridiculous, I don't care.* By the last votes I was thinking *I don't care who wins now, I just wish it was over.* It was very stressful. And then, 'Hurrah!' We won. I remember how Martina grabbed me around the neck and pulled my earring off. I could see Evelyn, about forty people back with the powder.

In a nail-biting finish, Ireland beat the UK's Sonia on the final vote. They couldn't have scripted it better. Despite this, Sonia was gracious in defeat and enjoyed her time here:

> It was a fantastic time for me to be asked by the BBC. It's for your country, and the three hundred million people watching you. It was fabulous; the whole experience was wonderful. We had a ball in Ireland. We partied every night.

For Niamh, it was an opportunity to go back on stage to a fantastic reception:

> All I could think about was that I had to sing again. So I walked out on stage. The three backing singers had had a bit of champagne, and the adrenaline was high. Nobody tells you what to do in that scenario; you never practise for that. I went over to the orchestra, and it felt like everybody's win. Every-

one was singing 'Ole! Ole! Ole!' I wasn't anywhere near the prize-giving spot and went to completely the wrong place. I wasn't anywhere near to where Linda was giving Jimmy the prize. Time was of the essence, so I had to be pulled straight back to sing. I missed the prize-giving, and you could see at the very end, when I was performing, that there were a huge number of photographers behind the line cameras. The minute the show was over they ran onstage. Either Patricia or Martina fainted as we were so squashed during the setting up of the press conference. You have so much to do once you win. That was only the beginning of the work. We had a press conference followed by a posh party for the big boys. I didn't get back to the Europa until about 3 AM. Meanwhile, my parents went back to the house. The neighbours and all the local people in Banteer had decorated the place. They brought a TV and the entire town wathced the Eurovision with my parents and family and had a party.

CHAPTER SIX
HAT-TRICK HEROES

With Ireland about to host its second Eurovision in succession, (the first country to do this), interest in song submissions increased even further. Dubliner Paul Harrington's first memory of the Eurovision was watching Sean Dunphy on an old black and white Murphy Digital Television. The three TV events that stood out for him in his formative years were the assassination of JFK in 1963, a man walking on the moon in 1969 and Dana winning the Eurovision in 1970. He frequented the same video library (Metropolis on Baggot Street) as Johnny Logan in the 1980s, but it wasn't until he entertained the performers and delegates after their rehearsals in the Eurovision Club in 1988 that he first became absorbed in the contest. He even managed to sing a duet with Celine Dion that week. After his solo album in 1991, he met up with Brendan Graham. Paul explains:

> The Eurovision came to me in a mysterious way. I had de-
> moed songs for Brendan Graham. We just met and got on
> well at an IMRO meeting or something. One of the songs
> that he asked me to demo was 'Rock 'n' Roll Kids'. I did,
> and he entered it. It didn't get through one year, then it did.
> He asked me whether I would perform it at the National
> Song Contest. I didn't really want to at the time, because I
> had a solo career going with a hit album and a hit single.
> There was people around me asking whether that would be
> cool thing to do.I remember thinking of calling him to say,
> 'I'm not going to do it', and he'd have had a big teddy bear
> smile on his face and would have said 'Well?' Eventually I
> said, 'Sure why not.' It was a fantastic gift as well. Brendan

asked me how would I feel about someone joining me, maybe playing guitar. Brendan had a very specific idea of how he wanted the song presented. He wanted to keep it simple, so I said, 'Yeah maybe some guitar would be nice.' He'd been writing with Charlie at the time, and I had seen Charlie with a band called Jargon in the National Stadium. I was impressed, and I'd loved a song called 'Bailieboro and Me'. I said, 'Yeah that'd be great.' And, as they say, the rest is history.

The National Stadium was where 'Rock 'n' Roll Kids' had its origins. Brendan was attending a Fats Domino gig there in 1991 when he got the inspirational song title. He got a lend of a Parker 51 pen from a Coopers and Lybrand employee, and wrote the song title on his ticket stub.

When he originally wrote the song it had four verses, one for the sixties, seventies, eighties and nineties. When he played it on his piano at home in Carrickmines to RTÉ DJ Ken Stewart, Ken told him that it was a great song, but too long. Brendan dropped the last two verses. Charlie McGettigan remembers doing a demo of 'Rock 'n' Roll Kids':

It goes back to about '92. Brendan had written the song, and he was over at my house and played it and asked if I would do a demo of it. I did a demo of it, but it was kind of Don Williams. We weren't thinking of the Eurovision at all. I was into country music at the time, and my demo was a kind of country music version of it.

Sandy Kelly remembers hearing that demo:

Back in 1992 when I went to Branson, Missouri to work with Johnny Cash, I brought 'Rock 'n' Roll Kids' to him as a demo from Brendan Graham. I played it to him and he listened to it, but he didn't get it. I could see him singing that with Willie Nelson and Waylon Jennings, like a Highwayman type thing. Every time I see Charlie and Paul singing it, that's the first thing that comes into my head, how I played it for Johnny Cash. I don't think Paul and Charlie even know that.

Brendan Graham had already had two bites at the cherry in 1976 and 1985. His nine-year itch was back again, but, as Brendan explains, it wasn't coordinated like that:

I entered it for '92, it didn't get through. I entered it for '93, it didn't get through. Before that you could enter as many songs as you liked. At that stage it had gotten down to one song. Before 'Rock 'n' Roll Kids' I'd written songs with the Eurovision in mind, somewhere in the intervening period I'd just write songs that I liked even if they weren't Eurovision songs, and just entered them. I felt strongly about 'Rock 'n' Roll Kids'. When I originally wrote it it had seven verses in it. I wanted to go through the sixties, seventies, eighties, nineties, and I remember playing it to Ken Stewart (who used to be on the radio) and he said 'That song is going to be a hit but it has too many verses.' I just really liked the song, and I said 'I'll send it in again'. I had already been knocked back twice with it.I was driving in the car one day and I heard this voice on the radio, and the song was 'What I'd Say'. I just thought *That guy has such a fantastic voice, a soulful voice.* I just remembered it and thought, *With this song, he's the singer.* At the time I didn't know what a phenomenal piano player he was, so I was lucky he agreed to the demo, and then agreed to do it. My notion is that everything is built from the song up, it would still be my notion. Some people shoehorn the song to fit the artist. I never see it that way, and I never write with an artist in mind. Get the song first and then pick who sings it.

Charlie takes up the story:

Brendan came back to me a year later, in '93. He had this version by Paul, and it was a really great version. It was just Paul and the piano, and I happened to be on the judging panel that year in 1993. I was sitting there, and the songs

123

come in unidentified. As soon as I heard it I knew it was Brendan and I had to say to the other people, 'Well I know who this is, so I'll have to abstain.' The song never got through.

Brendan never gave up on the song, and had faith in it and sent it in again for '94. He recalls:

The third year I sent in as a very simple demo with Paul Harrington on vocals and piano, and for a number of years before that I had this notion, as bells and whistles were starting to creep into the Eurovision, that if I had the right song I could keep the whole thing trimmed down to the bones. The song had to be really strong, and it's something I practise on a lot of my demos: just piano and voice. With piano and voice you can put on the army brass band, the orchestra and everything else, but it still won't work. So I began to look at songs and tone them down lower, chip them to the bone. With 'Rock 'n' Roll Kids', I said, 'Let's go back to the start, with just Paul and the piano for the demo.' It got through and I decided that I wanted to keep it this way, but I decided that sending one singer out on his own with a piano was demanding. I knew Charlie with his style of singing and I thought, *These two guys will gel, their voices will complement each other.* I knew that Charlie played very tasty acoustic guitar so I thought that would be it, just piano and acoustic guitar. I suggested it to Paul, and he was very generous. He said yes, then I contacted Charlie and he also said yes.

Charlie remembers Brendan asking him to come on board with Paul:

I wasn't on the judging panel the following year [1994], and Brendan put it in and it qualified. I had told him not to go putting orchestras or a big production on it, that the song would stand up with just the piano. He thought it needed something else, and asked whether I would be interested collaborating with Paul. It was a bad year for me, the ESB power station where I was working in Arigna had closed down, and we were moving to Donegal. I asked him if he really wanted me to do it, and he said, 'We really think this will work if you go in with Paul.' I relented after three days of persuading, and said, 'OK, I'll go with it.' I'd literally never met Paul before, though he seems to remember meeting me at some point. I remember we met in Westland Row. We sat down and gelled immediately, with him on the piano and me on guitar. We sang it once without any rehearsal whatsoever. We produced it, just the two of us, and went out that night to do *The Pat Kenny Show* and that was it. We rehearsed in the afternoon and sang it on *Kenny Live* that night. People were telling me what a great song it was. I said 'It couldn't be great, it's only himself and myself on the piano.' All I can remember is that the Maynooth Choir were on that night, and they thought it was brilliant. I was so chuffed that the Maynooth Chamber Choir thought it was great. I remember the year before going up to rehearse for the National Song Contest in that big studio in RTÉ, and walking in as Niamh Kavanagh was singing 'In Your Eyes'. I didn't really know her, and though *Jaysus, there's Niamh Kavanagh, fuck me, what a singer*. I didn't know at that stage that she'd be handing over the prize to us. I had no idea we were going to win.

Brendan's gut feeling paid off:

I knew that Paul would be absolutely right for it and I knew Charlie would be absolutely right for it, so I decided for the National Song Contest not to get any arrangement done at all. I saw the song as a small song, as a conversation in the kitchen, and I wanted the listeners to be drawn into that kitchen and into that conversation. I didn't want any distraction, and I felt the group was strong enough. I felt that the storyline was strong enough, and that it was also the kind of storyline that I knew people might be able to relate to, as life goes on, as time goes by and as love changes while the nostalgia for youth remains.

Just like the 1993 Eurovision, RTÉ headed back to Munster for the 1994 NSC final. Limerick's University Theatre was the venue on the night. Brendan remembers them running away with it:

> You hope you'll do well. We had a good feeling about the song, the guys were fantastic, but I didn't expect what happened. It was a great night and great that the National Song Contest was taking place outside of Dublin, not asking people to come to Dublin but going out to them instead. We were euphoric the night afterwards. I remember straight afterwards that the guy who was in charge of Light Entertainment came over to me and congratulated me. He said, 'Well done, it's a wonderful song, but you'll of course have to make it an event song for the Eurovision.' I asked what he meant by that?' And he said, 'Well it's a big event.' I said, 'Well the secret with this song is that it's not an event song, it's a small song with a little storyline and that's how people are responding to it.' Then somebody also said, 'Well you'll have to use the orchestra at the Point.' I said it wasn't really an orchestra song, and we should be thinking about the song. Then he asked when I was going to get an arrangement done. I said, 'It's working.' I remember being called into a meeting in the RTÉ canteen shortly before the Eurovision, and being asked if I'd made up my mind about the arrangement. I said 'I have yeah, there isn't going to be one.' I think it was Charlie who said, 'Would you not even consider a string quartet?' I knew it was a big ask of them, for the two of them to go out on a stage the size of the Point in front of hundreds of millions of viewers and do this, but I thought that vulnerability was essential to the core of the song. I also love the notion that you don't have to be strictly in time with an orchestra, but that they could ebb and flow with each other, which they did, and they put in a phenomenal performance on the night. There was a tendency to dress the artists also up for the Eurovision. I didn't want to do it that year. I said, 'The song is about blue jeans and blue suede shoes, and so you can't have them dressed up.' In fairness to Anita Notaro [head of delegation] she was brilliant. She took everything on board. To me, the emphasis was always on the song. When the guys came out to sing in blue jeans and blue suede shoes it all matched up.

What's Another Year?

Paul recalls a moment during rehearsals:

> I enjoyed the fact that it was on home soil. There can be an awful disconnect when you're far away from home, so for me it was great to play to a home crowd. It was fantastic. I remember they were closely guarding the interval act. That was going on all week. I also remember that we weren't using the orchestra, and at our first rehearsal we went out and they had a rather puny piano onstage. I said to myself, *I don't want to be awkward or difficult, and I certainly don't want to come across as a prima donna.* Eventually I said, 'This is not gonna cut it as a piano, give us a full size grand.' It was particularly because we weren't using an orchestra. The piano was quickly moved out and changed. It all went very smoothly after that.

Brendan remembers the build-up and the interval act:

> We actually stayed in the Berkeley Court Hotel – they were probably afraid we'd get lost. I remember how that morning Dickie Rock rang to wish us all good luck. Lots of people sent us lovely messages. It was great to be in our hometown, but I didn't want to go into the dress rehearsals. Bill Whelan and I had been friends for many years. When he wrote the intro piece to *Riverdance* he played it for me, and I was totally gob-smacked. It was just something so out of the ordinary. I decided not to go into the rehearsal because I wanted to see it on the night. I met Bill coming out of the auditorium, and he said to me, 'You know you're going to win this hands down. I've heard all the songs, and they all have a lot going on for them, but people are forced to listen to your song.' I thought it was a very interesting observation. I don't normally do it, but I put a few pounds on the song, and said I'd give it to Gay Byrne's fund if it came up. And, of course, it did.

Bill Whelan did the interval music for the 1981 Eurovision and recalls how *Riverdance* was born:

In December 1993 Moya Doherty [Eurovision 1994 producer] rang me. We went and had a coffee on Baggot Street. I remember it well. At that stage in 1992, just to put this in context, I had done *The Seville Suite*, which involved Irish dance and Spanish dance. We had brought in a flamenco dance, and put the Spanish and Irish dance together. In 1993 I did *The Spirit of Mayo* to celebrate the Mayo 5000 festival. That again had a big choir, Anúna. Michael Flatley and Jean Butler also appeared at that concert. It was kind of logical then when Moya called me in December and said, 'Having looked at *The Spirit of Mayo* and what's gone on, would you do something as a centerpiece for the Eurovision, seven minutes long and involving Irish dance?' I said, 'Yeah I will.'

It didn't come out of the blue, of course. A lot of people think *Riverdance* just came out of the blue, but there was history, and a clear route to it. I sat down in December of '93 and started to sketch it. We brought in [Michael] Flatley, and I played the music to him. *Riverdance* always had odd timing, not quite the same as jigs and reels. We had a bit of back and forth on it before it was ready. We worked it up as a dance piece before I went into the studio in March '94, and recorded it with the orchestra. Then that became the single. I set out to write it in 1993. I started to demo it at home in early 1994, and wanted to make a record out of it as it was going to be in the centre of the Eurovision. It'll get out to a lot of people, and it was a chance for me to continue the work that I was doing and get it out as a single. So I went to the record companies and back to the people who had put money into *The Seville Suite*, and I said, 'I want to do a seven-minute single.' Everyone came back to me and said, 'Seven-minute singles don't happen. There's no money in this except the cost of running it, and there's no chance of making the money back,' so that was my response from the music industry and I was really frustrated.

Bill's next move would be life-changing. enabling him to create chart history and putting him on the road to success, not to mention a Grammy award:

I did a corporate thing the previous year for Church &

General. There was a guy who ran the PR there called Damien O'Neill, and I called him and said 'I've a project here that needs money.' He asked 'What is it?' and I said 'It's a seven-minute single for the Eurovision.' He said 'OK, what do you need?' And I said 'I need to record it and pay for the orchestra in the studio.' He said 'Send it over to me.' I had this bizarre situation of sending a demo over to an insurance company, then getting a call that afternoon that I'll never forget. It was Damien O'Neill, and he said, 'We've had a listen to that and we like it. It's going to be in the middle of the Eurovision, yeah?' And I said 'Yeah, and we're going to put out the single'. He asked, 'How much will it cost?' and I said 'I'm going to need ten thousand pounds for pressing it, paying the orchestra and releasing it. I'm going need 10k.' and he said 'Yeah, we can do that. Can we put a little logo on it?' I said 'Of course you can, you can put it anywhere.' So he gave me a cheque for 10k, made the record and paid the orchestra. I went back to Paul McGuinness and said 'Can we put this out on Mother Records?' I had no record label and he said, 'No we'll put it out on Son Records.' On the eighth of May 1994 I was driving to Shannon Airport with my friend Martin, on our way to Florida for a holiday. During the drive we were glued to the chart show with Larry Gogan, curious to find out what was number one. When we heard that 'Rock 'n' Roll Kids' was number two we couldn't work out what the week's chart topper would be. Then Larry announced that Riverdance had gone straight in at number one.

It would go on to sell almost one hundred and fifty thousand copies in Ireland, and become Ireland's second biggest selling single since chart sales were calculated in '92 (behind Elton John's Princess Diana tribute). It would spend more weeks at number one than any other single in the history of the Irish charts. Bill continues:

It was number one for eighteen weeks. The funny thing is that when the Eurovision and *Riverdance* hit the next day we had a single. We would not have had a single if Church & General had not put the money into it. RTÉ were not going

129

to put money into it. *Riverdance* was a single and available
and in the UK charts, and it kept the whole *Riverdance* thing
alive. It was being played on the radio, and people had the
single and were playing it in their homes. It was something
concrete to take away from the Eurovision, and that was an
important link between the end of the Eurovision and when
we got out to do that full show.

Tommy Nolan got to see *Riverdance* up close:

I got promoted to the position of staging master in April
that year. I was at the planning meetings in '94 when I first
heard *Riverdance*. It grabbed me and every time it was
rehearsed I went out to the front and looked at it. It blew
me away, it was unbelievable. I knew there was something
special about it. I went out and sat in the audience for that
show. It was packed. I have never heard anything like it
before or since.

Gay Byrne also witnessed this magic moment:

I was a member of the RTÉ authority by then, and I found
myself with all the other authority members in the front
row in the balcony, with Mary Robinson, who was president
at the time. I clearly remember *Riverdance* coming on and the
place going stark raving mad when they finished. The
famous music came to a standstill and the place erupted. I
thought the roof was going to come off the building. The
response, which we've seen again and again on television,
was spectacular.

Paul also remembers the interval act:

It's a strange thing. On a night like that, of such magnitude,
a bomb could have gone off in Dublin centre and we

wouldn't have known about it. Over the years the interval act has been filled with some good things and some bad things. It's all about utilising that time, like the Hot House Flowers did back in the eighties. You can't know. It's isn't like we thought that *Riverdance* was going to be a global thing on the night. We watched it in the green room and were gobsmacked. We all stood up, just as the the crowd instinctively did. It was just part of an incredible evening. The overshadowing just becomes a media thing. Over the years, the media, and RTÉ in particular, rewrite history. It has been done in documentaries by people who don't take the time to study the original story, and who don't have the knowledge. They write it from a completely different point of view. twenty years of *Riverdance*, twenty years of 'Rock 'n' Roll Kids', there's no comparison. We're singers, they're dancers. Maybe we should have sung 'Rock 'n' Roll Kids' at the interval of *Riverdance* for twenty years, but that's not the way it works. We only saw *Riverdance* on the night. Everybody was swept away after the rehearsal. That said, I had a similar wardrobe call as Michael Flatley. I thought he was the American guy who worked for wardrobe in RTÉ, because he used to help me out with my clothing and brushing down my jacket and was just being very nice. The Polish woman who performed after us, Edyta Górniak, was the only one I was worried about. She was an amazing singer and a gorgeous woman. I liked her, but I didn't want her to win. I thought, *We'll do as best we can and perform as best we can.* We knew we did. I felt that we'd hack up or not get a look in. My gut feeling was that it was a really beautiful song, and anyone in their right mind would certainly acknowledge it as that.

Charlie recalls that period in his life:

At that time your feet never touched the ground. Literally. It went from radio stations to press interviews to doing videos. It was a big chunk out of our lives. The fact that it was in Dublin was an added bonus. It was like a home game, and the excitement was amazing. People ask me whether I was nervous, but it was probably the most relaxed on a programme I've ever been in my life; we had no constraints.

Paul and I have never played the song the same way twice, and we weren't tied to a backing track. We just played it as we felt it. I had forgotten that sound of the crowd roaring until the first night we did that Eurovision Winners Show in the Grand Canal Theatre [October 2012]. We'd walk up the steps to come down to the stage. I'd say to myself *What the jaysus did I get myself into.* I was trying to remember all the Eurovision songs and it was a nightmare. I thought it was going to be a disaster. I'd get to the top of the stairs, the curtains would be pulled back and I'd feel exactly the same warmth that there was at the Point Depot. I could not believe it. It hit me straight in the face. It was great to be at home. It was so easy. There were so many parties the week of the Eurovision. I remember we'd a big Irish night in O'Shea's up there behind the Bord Gáis Theatre. I brought the gang up from Drumshanbo. They had a fantastic night and met everybody – the Pat Kennys and the Gerry Ryans. We had a wonderful night. It's all about the music for Paul and me. The music is the most important thing, and to be able to just do that song as we did with the piano and guitar.

Brendan Graham remembers that victorious evening:

I decided that I was going to sit out in the auditorium. I did not want to be in the green room with cameras in your faces when you're trying to look relaxed, so I sat out in the hall. It was fascinating to see it and to be a part of the audience. Of course then I didn't know when to go up on stage, when Cynthia and Gerry were looking for me. I'm glad I did it because it was such a thrill to be part of the audience and not the team. I did it that year and then I behaved myself for '96. I remember afterwards we were brought around to various venues in Dublin for post-Eurovision parties. We were brought on stage when the Paddy Cole band was on. My youngest was about twelve, and we were brought into Lillie's Bordello. It was great to win in your home country, and it was the third of three.

What's Another Year?

Paul, Charlie and Brendan would tour Europe to promote the single. Paul concludes:

> We were on aeroplanes every weekend for most of the year. We had a lovely time and a good laugh. I still have a gift from that person who was assassinated a couple of years ago. Her name was Benazir Bhutto, from Pakistan. There was a special dinner for her and her husband in Dublin Castle, where there was a lot of security. Charlie and I were performing four songs after dinner, and for one of them I decided to do 'Uptown Uptempo Woman' which was a huge hit for me a couple of years earlier. When we were introduced to Benazir Bhutto, she said, 'That was one of my favourite songs when I was in college in university in the UK.' The original version is by Randy Edelman. She immediately presented her hand to shake mine, so I didn't want to leave her standing there. I shook hands with her and that was that. Protocols are only there unless someone allows you to break them. It was actually her that broke protocol by putting her hand forward to be shaken.

At their twentieth anniversary gig in the Sugar Club in 2014, Charlie told a lovely story about Paul's late mother. He'd been in her house around the time of their success, and noticed that there was a radio on in almost every room, the bedroom, sitting room and so on. When he asked her about this she innocently explained, 'The more radios the song gets played on, the better.' At that same anniversary concert, Brendan made a fantastic speech about the origins of 'Rock 'n' Roll Kids'. The final paragraph of his speech is reproduced here with Brendan's consent:

> Fats Domino had 'long gone' back to Louisiana . . . but, as I stood on the stage at The Point Depot, through the applause and the cheers - I heard a sound roll in over the Liffey Banks – the sound of a rollin', rumbling piano . . . and, for a moment, I wasn't there. I was back in the stadium, back on Bourbon Street, on that steamy Dublin night in 1991. Thank you, Fats!

CHAPTER SEVEN
ORCHESTRAL MANOEUVRES

In 1995 Ireland became the first country to host the Eurovision for three consecutive years and Dublin became the first city to host two Eurovisions consecutively. Host Mary Kennedy would capitilise on this in her opening speech, when she joked, 'RTÉ is pleased to welcome you once again to the Point Theatre in Dublin for what has almost become the annual Eurovision Song Contest from Ireland.'

Eddie Friel would be Ireland's representative with the song 'Dreamin'', which had been drawn to perform second. No one in that position has ever won, but that was the least of his worries. The song would make headlines for sounding too similar to a Julie Felix song called 'Moonlight'. It did more than sound similar and the songwriters didn't help their cause by including the song title in their lyrics. This had a negative effect across Europe and resulted in a fourteenth place finish on the night. A year later the Parnassis Group would release an excellent album entitled 'Eurovision Me Arse' that would bring the alleged plagiarism in 'Dreamin'' to hilarious new heights. For Eurovision humour there's no better album. Eddie wasn't the only Irish performer at the Eurovision that night. One half of the Norwegian entry Secret Garden was Kildare's own Fionnuala Sherry:

> In 1994 Rolf came back as the Norwegian writer of 'Duet' by Elisabeth and Jan Werner Danielsen. He and I started talking when Rolf wrote that song. After the '94 entry we got together. I knew he had a huge past with the Eurovision, and had a win in '85. We nipped into the RTÉ Studios and played it ['Nocturne'] together and that was it. It was one

of the most beautiful melodies I'd ever heard. I thought, *What is this piece of music?* And that was it. He was very impressed with how I played it and wanted to work together. If Millstreet hadn't happened, 'Nocturne' wouldn't have happened. It took a week in Millstreet and Killarney, living in a hotel in Killarney and going to Millstreet every day. That's what inspired 'Nocturne'. 'Nocturne' was a result of the Irish stay, and not many people know that – that's a unique piece of information. So when I met him a year later he said, 'I have this melody that I wrote.' Our career was born during the Eurovision.

It wasn't all straight forward for Secret Garden. Norway takes their Eurovision very seriously, with several qualification rounds. Fionnuala explains:

We had no intention of entering the Eurovision Song Contest. The powers that be in Norway had asked Rolf to submit a song, and he said 'I'm working with an Irish girl.' We were working on an album and had at that stage pre-recorded a lot of songs, and one of them was 'Nocturne', and they were interested to hear what he was working on, and it was a guy in Norway, the producer who said: 'You have to do this with the Eurovision.' We couldn't see it, we thought he was crazy, and he thought for the voting, we should put words to it, which we did, and we said, 'We'll give it a crack anyway,' but we very reluctantly did, and we said 'We're gonna continue on with our album anyway. We'll finish the album, and we'll see with the Eurovision what happens,' and also we'd been topping the album around and going through all the demos.

In '94 I left the orchestra, which was a little bit scary. Towards the end of '94 I left a full-time job, and I went out to Rolf and we started working up there. No matter what, we were going to record the album, but by January we'd premiered it in the first round in Norway and it's much more of an event, it's not like *The Late Late Show* here where you enter on the night. This is a serious competition with jury votes, with public votes, phone in, and in my year they pre-selected it down to twenty songs and then each week you had two songs pitted against each other until you had ten songs. In the first round I'm on TV in Norway for the first time, nobody knows me, and I'm a violinist from Ireland playing a song that is going to go to the Eurovision and we thought, 'There's not a prayer,' and we got forty-nine percent and barely scraped in. We got through the first round only by one percent. It was really difficult and then we gathered some momentum and by the time we got to the national final in Norway, I think we won it with quite a good margin, but it wasn't a straightforward run.

From January to May, Rolf and Fionnuala worked on their album, running between Iceland, Norway and Denmark. They were going non-stop, so the Norwegian team didn't even have time to dress Fionnuala. She explains:

RTÉ showed me one outfit that they wanted me to wear for the Eurovision, and I thought, *Oh no*. They tried putting me in silly dresses. They did want us in some costume, but they could never catch me because I was never in a place where they could measure me or dress me. We were in the studio two days before the first rehearsal, and I hadn't even figured out what I was going to wear. The press and magazines in Norway were ringing up to ask and I didn't know as I hadn't thought about it. 'Nocturne' was the very last song we mixed as we flew into Dublin, just in time for the first day's rehearsal. I wore leather jeans that had been in my wardrobe for five years, with a white shirt over a black top. It caused controversy up in Norway that I wore leather trousers.

Though she was representing Norway, Fionnuala was delighted to be participating on home soil:

It's scary in one way because it's hard to step out in front of your own colleagues with the orchestra accompanying us. I was a big part of that when I was in the orchestra. It was strange – it could have gone either way. Everyone, the team in RTÉ and the orchestra, was so good, thankfully. They really got behind us and were so kind to us and really did take care of me during the week. They made sure that I was happy with the sound and the microphones, because playing an acoustic instrument in a competition like that is hard. You really need to get the right microphone, and you need to get the right sound people around you. I was blessed that Rolf had so much experience at the Eurovision. He knew how to handle things and work the week.

Someone else with plenty of experience was participating as part of the interval act this year. Brian Kennedy recalls:

We had won it again and Ireland was really gathering momentum. We were reinventing ourselves in front of our own eyes. *Riverdance* was suddenly taking off, and making that kind of thing sexy. Before that sort of thing had been seen as parochial and old fashioned. I was so proud that Mícheál Ó Súilleabháin asked me to come and be a part of that whole extraordinary showpiece because it involved the monks of Glenstal Abbey, the Brennan Sisters and Evelyn Glennie, the percussionist, and a lot of amazing people. It was certainly one of the first times I sang in Latin. Mícheál Ó Súilleabháin said, 'I have a piece of this song that I hear you singing.' I went down to Limerick to visit him, and we actually ended up at the altar of Glenstal Abbey. We did a little bit of recording there. We just went for it. He liked the tone of my voice. I think he liked that he could hear my accent – I sounded a bit Irish. It was one of the first times, just gathering confidence to be able to do something extraordinary for that coveted slot, the interval act. The pressure to follow *Riverdance* was enormous. It was quickly perceived by everybody. It was one of the first ever platinum records I ever got. People really loved it. It's such a busy schedule that you don't have much time to think about things. We got to watch the show, more from backstage than anything, because everything runs like clockwork.

While Fionnuala would continue Ireland's winning streak that year, unfortunately most of her family were not there to share her proud moment:

> None of my family were able to attend the show. It wasn't
> catered for like that. There wasn't even an option to bring
> my boyfriend at the time. When we were winning, my mum,
> young brother and some of my siblings drove to the Point.
> They tried to come in to see me, but couldn't get past secu-
> rity. That was the only regret, that I couldn't be with them
> that evening.

While some people in RTÉ may have been relieved that Ireland hadn't won once again, The *Sunday Tribune* headline the following morning summed it up: 'Half the glory, none of the cost.' For Fionnuala, though, there wasn't even time to celebrate:

> We had to fly back to Norway, and that was very hard. It was
> a disappointment as the whole night just consisted of inter-
> views and photographs. You don't really get to party because
> you're on call, you're just working. I remember that the next
> morning, at some godforsaken hour, another press call came
> through at around 8 or 9 AM. I obviously wanted to stay with
> my boyfriend and my family, and go off for the day and have
> lunch with them. There were strong arguments for me get-
> ting on a plane and going back to Norway and doing a press
> call the next day, and I said, 'There's no need.' Rolf wanted
> to go to get a car and drive over to the west of Ireland. We
> had worked for four or five months on the album, and had
> just come from it straight into that week. We were absolutely
> exhausted. We just needed time out, but we never got it. We
> were bundled back onto the plane to Norway. They said that
> there was going to be a press call that evening, but there was-
> n't. We flew up and there was nothing. It wasn't until the next
> day, and once we went back to Norway, that the album was
> launched. The next thing we knew, we were out touring in
> Tokyo. I think it was a year or two before we had a break. Rolf
> and I still joke that we have never actually celebrated the Eu-
> rovision win. We have never even tipped a glass of champagne
> to one another and said, 'Well done'. It's just one of those
> strange things.

In May 2015 Secret Garden had planned to mark their twentieth anniversary with concerts in Rolf's hometown of Kristiansand, but Fionnuala suffered a bad fall in Dublin in February, which resulted in her breaking bones in both hands. She had to undergo surgery and prolonged physio, but thankfully made a full recovery to perform three concerts in Kristiansand that August.

After three very successful Eurovisions in Ireland, Norway got the honour of hosting the Eurovision in 1996. With Eurovision-mania having gripped the emerald isle for three consecutive years, comedy writers Graham Linehan and Arthur Mathews decided to capitilise on the attention and devoted a full episode of their second series of 'Father Ted' to the Eurovision. Featuring Frank Kelly, Dermot Morgan and Ardal O' Hanlon. The 'Song For Europe' episode featured the priests performing an obscure Norwegian Eurovision B-side song entitled 'My Lovely Horse' (accompanied by a Swarbriggs-inspired video) and entering it into the NSC. Declan Lowney was the director:

> At the script stage there was confusion over what a National Song Contest was and how the Eurovision was structured. I helped the guys structure it. I don't think Graham would have ever sat through an actual Eurovision. The guys pretty much wrote everything that was there, including the ludicrous video with the horse. Graham knew Neil [Hannon] and I think they wanted to use a different song. Jeffrey Perkins said, 'No, use that one, ['My Lovely Horse'] it's great.' 'My Lovely Horse' was all Neil. Graham wrote the lyrics as well, and they had it all in their head.

Brendan Graham wasn't finished with the Eurovision yet, and had another ace up his sleeve. He recalls:

> I entered 'The Voice' in 1995. It didn't get through, but again people said to me, 'Why would you enter again? Your chances of winning are a zillion to one.' That was what ap-

pealed to me. I loved the notion that I might actually fail, so I had this other song that I was working on. In 1993 I became redundant. I was an industrial engineer, but decided to give songwriting a go. So I became a songwriter and started experimenting with songs. I also became interested in the history of the Famine, and decided to write a couple of connected songs, like those old-fashioned concept albums. The first of those that I wrote was 'Winter, Fire and Snow'. I had started writing 'The Voice' in 1993, before *Riverdance*. It was a very individual tune, different to anything I had done before. I was deciding where to go with it.

I was friends with Dervish and had done some bits and pieces with them. Dervish did a fantastic demo for me, with Cathy and the band. I loved it. I submitted that in 1995 and . . . nothing. So then, I thought, This is different. This is not a Eurovision song. I thought that f it got through it might do well, so I sent it in again. When I got word that it had gone through, I tried contacting Dervish since they had done the demo, but they were on tour. Because of 'Winter, Fire and Snow' I had gone to Anúna's Christmas Concert in St. Patrick's Cathedral and I'm sitting at the back and I can't really see the stage and all of a sudden I hear this voice out of heaven singing 'Winter, Fire and Snow' and I'm sitting there and then I saw this tall, beautiful, elegant young woman walk past me and I just thought, everything about this song 'The Voice', this is the voice I'm after, and as they were walking off stage I said to Mary [his wife], 'That's the singer, that's the singer.'

Eimear Quinn remembers that life-changing evening and takes up the story:

It was as a consequence of Anúna's involvement in *Riverdance* that I became involved with them. All their singers were involved in the touring *Riverdance* show, and they needed to increase their ranks so they could take on the Anúna concerts as well as sustain their *Riverdance* contract. They needed new soloists; that's when I joined. I joined Anúna the year after *Riverdance*, in Christmas 1995. I would have only been with them a couple of months. During their Christmas concert in St Patrick's Cathedral, Brendan Graham was in the audience when I sang his song, 'Winter, Fire and Snow'. That's when he approached me to see if I would sing 'The Voice' in the National Song Contest. It was a huge compliment. It was one of those moments that performers wait for their entire lives.

You want to make a connection with somebody in the audience who wants to collaborate with you, and you want it to be something that takes you in an entirely different and exciting direction. I wouldn't have known his history, other than that he was the man who wrote 'Winter, Fire and Snow'. I asked him, 'Are you sure you've the right person?' He said, 'I'm absolutely sure.' I was very much classically orientated at the time. I didn't really sing much folk music, or much beyond the classical genre, and I knew that this would have been the furthest away from classical music. He got me to sing the song a few times in the studio, and we listened back to the recording and made pointers about the expression, the pronunciation and so forth. He worked a fair bit with me on the interpretation of the song, and it was massively helpful. It was only after he did that with me, that I had the confidence to say, maybe I can do it justice.

With the singer in place, the next task was to build a group around Eimear. Brendan explains:

I wanted to have a band of real musicians again. I heard these classical musicians and contacted them, and they were up for doing it. That's how the band came about. They were an attractive looking bunch of people, but that's not why they were on the stage, it was because they were fantastic musicians. I thought, for this one, that I would need an arrangement, so I asked Bill Whelan, who did a phenomenal job. I had an instrumental part in the middle of it, but it was only in half-time. Bill came up with the fiddle solo, which was, I think, critical to the song, and helped it take off.

Bill Whelan remembers working on that one:

We did the demo of 'The Voice' in my attic, the same attic that I wrote *Riverdance* in. It's a lucky attic, I can tell you.

As Eimear recalls, there was no competition for Brendan's composition in the NSC:

I went into the National Song Contest singing, and I felt like a duck out of water. There were quite a few well established Irish performers and cabaret stars. I didn't have any of that experience, and I didn't know what I was doing. I had a desperate cold the night of the National Song Contest, and my voice wasn't at one hundred percent. To be honest, I was scared. I didn't think I was going to be able to bring Brendan's song any further than there. That National Song Contest was in the Point. RTÉ had just produced a fashion show the previous week for *Kenny Live*. The NSC used to be on *Kenny Live*, so they had the lease of the Point and decided to have the song contest there and make a big event out of it. It was more intimidating for a performer. The song was very strong. It was what won, really. It was a head and shoulders above all the other songs.

For the first time in four years, the Irish delegation headed abroad to participate. Brendan remembers the build-up:

There was a great line up that year. There were strong songs from Britain and elsewhere, but I think the one that we had was different again. We had an orchestra, and it wasn't a manufactured Eurovision song. The Oslo Spectrum was a huge arena. We also had to contend with Channel 4 making a fly-on-the-wall documentary. It was good, but quite intrusive. I remember, one time, when Noel Kelehan was making a telephone call in the lobby of the hotel, I saw this guy with a boom microphone dropping it in over him. I went over to this guy and said, 'That's a private conversation.' There was another time that we were having a band meeting with the producer Noel Curran, and I saw this microphone being stuck in the door as someone was coming in. You realise that they are looking for controversy. Something happened that has only happened to me once before. I remember sitting across from Eimear as the votes came in. I don't know what it was, I sensed what the votes would be from a number of different countries, and I remember predicting that we'd get a number of votes from such and such a country, and we did. I knew we had something special, and I knew the whole thing was right in every sense of the word. Hope is one thing, expectation is another. You never expect to win, and then it just seemed to happen. The votes kept coming in, and a few countries liked the song. The voting wasn't as consistent as for 'Rock 'n' Roll Kids' but we got a large number of points.

Eimear remembers meeting Morten Harket:

I was a huge a-ha fan. I was totally star-struck – he's gorgeous. Standing in the lift going up and down with Morten Harket was a real thrill. In my own head it was like I was fifteen and listening to 'Take On Me' or something. It was very strange. We were all sitting back and enjoying it and then the results started coming in. The song started to score really well and really pull away from the others. At that point I can't remember. It just became surreal. Someone recently drew my attention to a clip of me that somebody posted on YouTube, where Morten Harket came to our little space in the green room to talk to us in. He got me singing, and I sang 'Norwegian Wood' by The Beatles.

I actually have no memory of it whatsoever, probably because it was such a surreal experience. It was all a bit of the blue. What made it different for me was that it wasn't my area of expertise – I wasn't a pop, cabaret or lounge singer. I wasn't used to bright lights, glitz and showbiz, and I didn't have this planned career trajectory where I was thinking about the next big move. It's a massive opportunity for anybody. It was a massive opportunity for me, and one that I'll always be grateful for, but it wasn't something that had I worked towards. It all happened really fast, and I'd never planned on being there. It took me massively by surprise, so

I literally just took each moment as it came. I had no bigger plan, which left me free to enjoy it. I was looking on it as an experience. To be honest, unless you have an album ready to go and management ready to push everything and capitalise on the exposure, then really that's all it is. It's just a flash in the pan, and if you can enjoy it as that, then it's a good thing. I felt a bit bad about it – not that I didn't want to be there, but I felt like I had stolen someone else's dream. I felt like for so many people it would have been their master plan, while I was kind of an imposter.

Brendan was hugely impressed with Eimear's role as an ambassador for the country:

I remember thinking that Eimear was twenty-two or twenty-three and a student. I remember watching her in interviews and thinking how fantastic it was for the country to have someone like her as an ambassador. She was absolutely brilliant, how she portrayed herself. To me, she was everything that was good about the Irish. She was courteous, graceful, had a sense of humour and intelligence. She was a wonderful talent.

Having handed over the trophy over the previous year, Brendan found himself in the enviable position of getting it back. Fionnuala remembers Morten Harket and returning for the prize-winning ceremony:

I was a fan of a-ha. Morten is such a sweet guy and Kjetil Bjerkestrand is an amazing writer and composer and producer and keyboard player. He does all their arranging and their live shows with them. I actually got him to do my own solo album, which I did a few years ago [2010]. He was the person I chose to work with on that. He's amazing. We flew straight in from the States, and arrived on the afternoon of the show. I remember that we just had time to get to the hotel, change and then to the conference centre. I was there just in time to hand the prize to Eimear.

While accepting his prize, Brendan remembers one very special person:

> It was fantastic having Noel Kelehan on stage to share the
> moment with us. I got in trouble afterwards because myself
> and Mary had decided that win, lose or draw, we would head
> up to the most northerly part of Norway. I didn't realise
> how long a country Norway is. We headed off and weren't
> in the homecoming party. The Norwegians were wonderful
> and left us alone. I wasn't back for *The Late Late Show*. It
> wasn't a snub to them or the team, it was just something we
> decided we'd do. We had a holiday and saw the midnight
> sun. I remember sitting up all night to watch the sun go
> down but not below the horizon, then back up again. I
> watched from a fisherman's hut in the sea. I remember
> thinking, *I'm not going to bed until I see this.* The Norwegians
> are very hospitable, courteous people. They have something
> lovely about them.

For Eimear, the next natural step was to tour Europe and promote the single, but
that's not how it unfolded. Eimear explains:

> Brendan had the patience of a saint. There was a huge
> amount of interest in the song, which started in the UK.
> No Irish song had done this in a while. It went in at number
> forty. Polydor, who had licensed the song, were putting me
> under pressure to do loads of publicity, and were baffled
> when I wanted to sit my exams. Brendan, in fairness to him,
> said, 'You need what you need to do,' and didn't put me
> under any pressure whatsoever. He let me go and do my
> exams and after that I went on a bit of a tour with him,
> doing European TV and all that, but he did let me go and
> sit my exams. He was great. I'm sure he was tearing his hair
> out but he never let on. It was a mind-blowing experience.
> I'm not sure if I could have coped with any more of the
> showbiz, to be honest. I'd never done *Top of the Pops*. That
> was probably the one shot in my life that I regretted, but
> 'Top of The Pops' is gone now, anyway.

Eimear met Noel Curran [former Director-General of RTÉ] during the Eurovision, they started going out and later married. Eimear explains:

> We met through the Eurovision, and started going out shortly after I came back from Oslo. Noel was the producer of the National Song Contest in 1996 because he was the producer of *Kenny Live* at the time, and then the producer of the NSC. He went out to Norway as the producer of the Irish act and would sit in the box with the director of the Eurovision during rehearsals and make suggestions on lighting and so on. He travelled with the Irish delegation and when we won it, came back and produced the Eurovision in 1997 in the Point.

Brendan Graham would go on to have continued success following his Eurovision triumphs. He wrote several successful books. His most high-profile song would be 'You Raise Me Up'. He also later composed the lyrics to a Paul Mealor melody which became 'Sleep On' and was dedicated to Prince William and Kate Middleton's first child. He also wrote 'The Fair Fair Land'.

In 2015 he collaborated with the legendary David Foster on '*Stare Con Te* (Once Upon Love)'. Forty years on from his first Eurovision adventure, Brendan's appetite and enthusiasm for a great song remains undiminished.

For the fourth time in five years, Ireland was once again hosting the Eurovision. Yet again, the event was held in the Point Depot. The Irish representative, singer-songwriter Marc Roberts grew up in Crossmolina, County Mayo. Before his big break in 1997 he had already submitted songs. Marc recalls:

> It was Johnny McEvoy who encouraged me. He said, 'Look you're a writer, why not send something in?' I remember sending something in that, in hindsight, was quite like 'The Streets of New York'. It didn't have a hope in hell of getting into the competition. I suppose it was just the idea that had sown a seed in my mind. There's nothing else, as a songwriter, that you can do. Then 'Mysterious Woman' came about. John Farry had this song and Charlie McGettigan said that if he was looking for somebody to sing it, I was the man to do it.

It was originally called 'European Woman'. He reworked it to become 'Mysterious Woman'.It had already been entered at least twice before. I recorded it. It was a full arrangement. I recorded 'Mysterious Woman' then forgot about it. It was just me and a piano. That was what was entered into the National Song Contest. I then got the call from John Farry to say that the song had been accepted, and would be one of the finalists on the 'Pat Kenny Show' ['*Kenny Live*'] at the time.

The Eurosong finals were held in the Regional Technical College in Waterford and included Gary O'Shaughnessy and Maggie Toal, who'd participated in previous finals. The interval act, Parazone, was probably what most people remember. It featured Brendan O'Carroll and The Swarbriggs in white suits doing a parody of Boyzone. Marc remembers the final:

During the rehearsals Brendan O'Carroll sat down in the audience and watched the whole thing. My manager, Don, was sitting in the audience. As soon as I sang – I was the last to sing – Brendan O'Carroll legged it. After the show, when I won, Brendan came up to me and said 'I've won a fortune and I'm delighted.' He had gone off to Paddy Power's and put money on me after watching the rehearsals. Darren Holden came second. It was a gallop to the end with the two of us.

Marc remembers having other things on his mind around that time:

I was about to be signed by Ritz Records. They were, from my point of view, taking forever. As a young singer-songwriter you just want to get on with it. In hindsight I suppose they wanted to hinge the launch on something. I told them, 'I've been asked to do this,' and how it was more exposure. As soon as that happened they went into negotiations to sign me straight away. I knew I had got what I wanted – to finalise a record deal – so that was exciting. Johnny Logan was in the audience, there with my mam and dad. During

the intermission he said, 'You're definitely going to win it.'
He partied the night away with us. It kind of closed the
whole thing full circle, as I had met him as a kid. I got up
the next morning at about 7:45 AM, and I had an interview
with every radio station in the country. I remember walking
into the breakfast room in the Towers Hotel in Waterford
to a round of applause, and there was a colour photograph
of me in the *Irish Times*. I remember turning on my phone
and there being no room for messages. That's when it hit
me. Then I had to go and do a broadcast with Larry Gogan.

Then I had to go to the Waterford studios and do a
live link-up with Marty Whelan and Ciana Campbell. It was
full on publicity, which was great. I didn't listen to any of
the twenty-six songs. I remember doing *The Late Late Show*
the week before. I hadn't met Gay Byrne before that. I went
out and sang the song and Gay came straight over and interviewed me. He said, 'You're tipped to win,' and I said
'Yeah apparently so, but I made a conscious decision not to
listen to any of the songs.' He asked why and I said, 'So that
I don't feel like anyone is better than me.' He started laugh-
ing, and the record company were thrilled. He talked to me
about my songwriting and how there was one for everyone
in the audience – a CD, not a Marc Roberts!

The week of the Eurovision turned into pandemonium. As Marc recalls:

One of the tabloids rang me and said, 'How do you feel about
the coded message?' I said, 'What message?' They said, 'The
IRA have sent a coded message to say that a bomb was going
to go off in the Point Depot at 8:20 PM,' the time I was due
to go out on stage. I pretended to know about it, and they
asked how I felt about all the security that would be around,
and whether I thought about how it would feel for people
coming from all over the world being searched when they
arrived. I said that it was in everyone's interest that we have
security. He said goodbye and hung up. I turned to my
manager and just said, 'A coded message?' The Point was
emptied out a few times two or three days beforehand, and
sniffer dogs were brought in. The organisers were quite
happy, but on the night, at twenty minutes past eight, every-

one became a little nervous. I had enough on my mind. I
thopught, *I've got to sing anyway, and if it explodes, it explodes.*

Marc's moment had arrived. He remembers every single minute of it:

The general consensus in RTÉ was that they would close if
we won. One of the head guys in RTÉ came up to me
before I went on stage and said, 'Get out there and win it.'
They'd made a deal with BBC Northern Ireland or UTV. I
remember the last few steps walking up onstage, it was like
boiling hot oil. The crowd went mad. Mary Robinson was
president at the time. She was from Ballina and I was from
Crossmolina, which was lovely. Pat Kenny waved at me from
his little box, and I looked down into the audience and saw
my sister and her husband and Don and his wife. I thought,
Grand, you can do this, you've waited a lifetime for it. I remember
Denis Byrne was the floor manager. He came up to me,
straightened the microphone and said, 'Are you all set Marc,
are you ready to take part?' He walked away, and the music
started.I always wanted to perform with an orchestra, but
this was the very first year that they brought in backing
tracks. As a result, we had the orchestra as the backing track
to the song. All vocal tracks have to be live, but we all sang
live to the backing track. Frank McNamara was the musical
director, but unfortunately he'd nothing to do with us. Noel
Curran was the director. They were a lovely bunch of
people.

The voting was close and Ireland and the UK were neck and neck. In the end, Ireland's grip on the Eurovision crown was over. Katrina and The Waves won with
'Love Shine a Light', and Marc had to be content with a runner-up spot:

I always feared coming second last rather than coming
second. The fact that we had won so many times made me
feel that it could go either way. It opened all the doors for
me, and my connection with the Eurovision will always be
there. I'm proud of it and it's what I wanted. At the end of

the day it's an amazing opportunity to represent your country. It's one of those competitions that nobody says they watch, but then it's in every conversation. Everybody watches it. After that it was gas. The following morning I signed my record contract. The following Monday we were on *Richard and Judy* in the UK and then the song hit the UK charts. It all hinged on 'What's it like to represent a country that didn't want to win?'

Marc also remembers the song being in the charts:

It reached number two in the Irish charts, kept off by 'I Believe I Can Fly'. Week after week it was R. Kelly. The record company would ring me up during the week and say, 'Who is this R. Kelly?' President Mary Robinson requested to meet me. The people who were head of my delegation said that I was too busy and couldn't meet her. I was so angry at the time. I remember Ronan Keating and Carrie Crowley were sent out to meet her and I really wanted to. I felt really bad about that and ended up doing a couple of functions. I met President Robinson and told her. She invited me, my mum, dad and my manger Don to a function in *Áras an Uachtaráin*. She was sorry that it didn't work out at the time. I've performed many times since then at events with President Michael D. Higgins, both at compered functions and in *Áras an Uachtaráin*. It is the fact that President Robinson was from Mayo and that I was from Mayo that I would have loved for it to have happened.

Little did we know then, but Marc's performance in 1997 would be Ireland's last top five appearance to date. The following year, Dawn Martin was Ireland's representative in Birmingham. There was controversy before the event when RTÉ ditched Dawn's original backing singers, sisters Elaine and Karen Matthews, in favour of singers who knew the ropes. Paul Harrington explains:

Dawn got through. Graham Murphy and Chris O'Brien produced her song. Graham was playing accordion on stage with Eddie Friel. I had done a lot of backing vocal work for them. Myself and a girl called Karen Hammill did the backing vocals on that particular record. RTÉ decided, as all the vocals had to be live in the Eurovision, that her backing vocalists weren't strong enough to perform on the night. They asked myself and Karen to do the gig in Birmingham and it was great. It was one of the best gigs I'd had in years. We were reporting to the *Pat Kenny Show* every day, and having a bit of fun and meeting the gang at night. We met Terry Wogan and all sorts of characters. The guy from Right Said Fred [Richard Fairbrass] was making a documentary of it. There was no pressure to deliver, just to do your job. I had no difficulty with that. I like singing. I remember meeting Katrina (from the Waves) and her being particularly unfriendly. In the commentary box, I don't think people even mentioned that I was there, for the simple reason that they didn't want to detract from Dawn's performance. I had no difficulty with that, and I was very welcomed that week.

CHAPTER EIGHT
MILLENNIUM PRAYERS (2000-2009)

As the Eurovision moved into a new millennium, Monaghan singer Eamonn Toal, from Castleblaney, capitilised on the occasion. His father, Tommy 'Fat Sam' Toal sang with the Maurice Lynch Showband and also with Paddy Cole. Eamonn, though, was more interested in sport than the music business. That changed in 1990 when his father died suddenly onstage in front of thousands of people. Eamonn started rehearsing with a rock band in London and began to write the musical chapter in his life. In 1995 he got his first taste of the Eurovision when Frank Mc-Namara asked him to sing backing vocals for Eddie Friel in Dublin. Eamonn explains how he got involved in 2000:

> I was basically plucked from obscurity for the National Song Contest. I was recording in Drogheda for one of the song-writers – Gerry Simpson [brother of the late Spyder Simpson]. He co-wrote the song with Raymond Smith from Raheny, Dublin. I was recording some songs and Gerry said, 'We need that man for our song.' It was the week of the final and we had contractual issues. I had to get the lawyer and solicitor because they wanted a contract in case we won. They said they'd pull the song if I didn't sign the deal. I'm not saying that in a negative way, that's just the world of the music business. It was an amazing evening. It was so fitting that, on the night, Paddy Cole was the penultimate judge to give the regional votes. He gave me the votes that actually won it and made it mathematically impossible, with still a vote to go, for anyone else to win. I got about five maxi-

mums from the six regionals. Keith Duffy was waiting to give the final vote, hoping it would be exciting, but it was irrelevant.

While Eamonn was the winner, it was actually third place Shimma (featuring Bertie Ahern's daughter, Cecelia) headlined the following day. The *Evening Herald* went with the headline 'Cecelia Scoops The Plaudits From Eurosong Night'. That didn't bother Eamonn, though – he was the one on the plane to Stockholm and the sixteen-thousand capacity Globe Arena.

> As soon as we walked in for our first rehearsal on Tuesday, the German team, with Stefan Raab, chorused 'Celebrate the new millennium of love, ladies and gentlemen we have the Irish team.' This was in the green room and it was amazing. I didn't even know who he was. It was a compliment to our song, our pedigree and our history in the competition. I couldn't even say what their song was at the time, but they had a skit at the Eurovision, taking the piss out of it. On Saturday morning I was overcome. I got the shakes, something that I had never experienced before. I went back to my room and didn't want to see anybody. I spoke with my wife, and managed to focus and talk myself out of it, which was a strange experience. I didn't want to repeat that night, so I went out so calmly that you could see it in my performance. There wasn't a shake in my hand.

Eamonn attended all the parties during the week and mingled with the various delegations, but it was his adopted hometown of Dunshaughlin that he most wanted to impress with his performance. He didn't disappoint. His sixth place finish would be our best result this century, and his homecoming emphasised that. There were two hundred people at the airport wearing T-shirts with his face emblazoned on them, an open-top bus and police escort to Dunshaughlin where there were over five thousand fans waiting. He was also the guest of honour at a parade in Castleblaney and the *Sunday World* headline read 'Still Our Number One'. It's an experience Eamonn will never forget:

I'm one of about fifty people to represent my country. It was exposure that you couldn't buy. We met Terry Wogan on the day of the Eurovision, and he quoted words from our song. When he introduced the song he said, 'You're going to like this Irish song, there's a line in it that goes: "Our footprints leave a harvest for the children."' The exposure I got was amazing, especially for someone like me, who was just breaking into the music business. It is something that will stay with me forever.

The Eurosong just wasn't producing songs that European countries could identify with and RTÉ was looking at alternative ways to find a good song. With reality TV dominating the screen, RTÉ ran with a formula similar to programmes that had been running in the UK and America. Singers and songwriters would audition for a panel of judges and get their five minutes of fame on national TV. Mickey Joe Harte explains how he got involved:

As a songwriter and musician, the Eurovision was always on my radar, not because I wanted to do it but just because other songwriters do it. You would talk to people who entered it. A good friend of mine used to be a backing vocalist and we were always talking with people about Ireland's Eurovision legacy. As a songwriter it was always there, but it was never a real aspiration of mine. I was more influenced by the rock 'n' roll end of things. I didn't know anything about competition to enter it. My mam rang me. Her sister had been ringing and was saying 'They have this competition and they are in Derry today, why doesn't Mickey go down for it?' She knew that I was into that. I'd done a lot of these competitions in the past, but I had no intention of doing anything like that as I had just been in Nashville the previous year. I had a manager in place, we had an EP ready to go and all the artwork was done.

My wife asked me to go down, just to get some peace from my mum and aunt. Louis Walsh and Phil Coulter were involved, and Darren Smith from EMI Records. I knew there were some heavyweights in that regard. I thought that maybe I could get a song or get picked for something else,

155

or that I might get Louis's phone number. That was all. I went down and did the audition. I was the very last person in the last group of four or five. It was very late, and I just jumped in the car afterwards and headed to a gig. I got a call the next day to say I'd gotten through to the next round. Then I got through to the TV part of it. I rang my manager and said, 'You might kill me but I just tried out for this thing.' He said, 'Maybe it'll be no harm, we might get a few weeks exposure out of it and it'll help.' Then it mushroomed from there.

I can't for the life of me remember exactly what I had planned the day I went there. I think it was a Police song or something. I was talking to one of the researchers, Niamh. She was a cool girl and into her music. She asked if I knew any Bob Dylan and I told her I loved Bob Dylan and that I could do a version of 'I'll Be Your Baby Tonight'. She said that the panel hadn't heard any Bob Dylan songs, and that they might get something from it. I thought it seemed like a good plan, so I went in and sang that. It was Niamh who put me in that direction. It was something I was able to go in and do an interpretation of on the guitar, which helped a wee bit.

Little did Mickey know that he was putting himself in line to represent Ireland at the Eurovision Song Contest. Maybe even RTÉ didn't even know. He explains:

I was halfway through the competition and somebody said to me, 'You know, if you win this, you'll go and represent Ireland at the Eurovision.' It was so far away at that stage that I didn't even think of winning it. Although I was in the heats and the final, I never thought it was going to be me. The closer it got, the more I started to think about it. I have a funny feeling that it was only as a result of the success of the show that RTÉ made the decision. They would obviously never admit that, but that's my take on it. Now, with hindsight, there was never a whisper of the Eurovision. Because of the success now it's huge and we'll get a few months out of it. We'll get one really good song and we'll have the whole nation behind it. It'll be a great way of injecting a bit of spark into the Eurovision, and there'll be a whole new interest in it.

Mickey had worked with Louis Walsh before when he was in a band called Reel. They were like a young version of the Clancy Brothers with an acoustically contemporary folk sound. It never quite worked for them. Phil Coulter had found a song that he wanted Mickey to sing in the final, written by Martin Brannigan and Keith Molloy. They had a good track record with B*Witched, Boyzone, and even Ant & Dec. The final of *You're a Star* came down to two people: Mickey and Simon Casey. Mickey remembers that time with mixed emotions:

> I think the final of *You're a Star* was pretty close. I always felt, and other people felt it too, that Simon was going to win. Louis had been on his side and Brian McFadden was his mentor and had written a song for him. He had a big Westlife following, and it was very close when I won. About six weeks later I had to go to the Eurovision, but my dad died just at the start of April. It was a crazy thing to happen in the middle of that and I came off the back of a humungous thing. Everybody wanted a piece of me and then my dad died. He was ill for a while but at least the good thing was, he got to see me winning the show, he had a degree of consciousness, but he was still very ill. We'd a few scares before that and it just happened between things.
>
> Funny enough, I was over and back to London recording with producer Jon Kelly and that morning I was just going back to London to record some more. We were trying to get the album done in-between and my dad was in Lifford Hospital and my mum said 'Go and see your dad, he's not very well today,' but he'd been up and down so much, it was just one of those things, oh he's down again. I went down that day and he died when I was there believe it or not. It happened in-between, a bit of a rollercoaster of emotions to say the least.

Mickey then hat to travel to Riga:

We had fantastic support. There was a chartered flight that came out from Derry and there was about three hundred people in the hall, and another chartered flight came out from Dublin, with all the connections of the two songwriters and all my connections up in the north west, so I had huge support and a lot of them said it was the best time they ever had. The morning of the Eurovision I got a good luck message from Johnny Logan put under the door of the bedroom, which was very nice and I got others also. I performed third on the night, just ahead of Sertab Eraner. I think it was a surprise winner, although she was a Sony artist in Turkey. She had a very substantial fan base and they were networking as well and she put in a good live performance. They were in the dressing room right beside us. And t.A.T.u. were there and we had great craic in rehearsal. Were they gonna kiss on stage? Which they didn't in rehearsals. It was much ado about nothing. During my performance, my eye started stinging because of the make-up and people were asking me, 'Were you crying because of your dad?' and I was saying 'No, it was because of the mascara or the eyeliner.'

Due to the increase in entrants in recent Eurovisions, the EBU had to make changes. From 2003 there would be a semi-final to accommodate the extra countries taking part, so Mickey knew a top-eleven finish would guarantee Ireland automatic entry into the next year's final. He achieved that:

Once I knew that I wasn't going to win, I just thought, *If I can go home after enabling them to qualify automatically for next year, I'll be happy*. Thank God I got that much out of it. I was very disappointed for Gemini and I met the girls' mother afterwards. They were from Liverpool. They were very nice, and certainly didn't deserve to come last. I think there was a problem with their monitor. There didn't seem to be a great UK presence with them from the BBC, they seemed to be left to do a lot of the stuff by themselves.

Despite finishing outside of the top ten, Mickey would go on to reap the rewards with the release of the single and album, giving him a double chart-topper in Ireland, beating the likes of Meatloaf and Black Eyed Peas:

> Having the biggest selling single of the year in Ireland wasn't something that was planned, it was just something that happened. It's a nice thing to have, because you don't know how people are going to react when it's released. It's different now. If you sold now what you did then you'd stay in the charts for a whole year. The ends justified the means. Something you're always struggling with throghout the Eurovision thing is your credibility as a songwriter. I'm still working away and try to get out and work whenever I can and that's the way you can get people's opinions and get your songs out there and that's always at the top of the agenda.

Following the tsunami in Asia on St Stephen's Day in 2004, Brian Merriman put together a fund raising event that saw one hundred percent of the proceeds go to the victims. With Linda Martin's help, they rounded up several people connected with the Eurovision and put on a fantastic show in Dublin in January 2005. Linda recalls:

> We could have sold out a week in the Olympia on that gig. There were people standing and sitting in the aisles. The demand for tickets for that Eurovision gig was incredible.

The show was presented by Mary Kennedy and Carrie Crowley. Some artists were unable to make it and sent video messages. On the night, the show featured Linda, Niamh, Paul and Charlie, Twink, Eimear, Shirley Temple Bar, Chris Doran, Mickey Harte and Brendan O'Carroll who sang 'Walking The Streets in the Rain'. It was a fantastic evening and a resounding success.

In 2005, sister and brother, Donna and Joe McCaul, participated at the Eurovision in Kiev, but failed to qualify for the final. While it's easy to knock any performer who doesn't do well, we have to remember that they are only human. When the semi-final ended there was a woman who was inconsolable: Mrs

McCaul, proud mother to Donna and Joe. While the media might have a go at them, they were still someone's children and only teenagers.

Joe continued to dabble in the music business, and later appeared in *The X-Factor* television show. Donna returned to the Eurosong final in 2010 doing what Mickey Harte had done. She dropped the 'Joe'.

In 2006, RTÉ decided to run with a formula they hadn't tried since the seventies. Back then, both Tina and The Swarbriggs were chosen to perform all songs in the final. Essentially, the performer was chosen before the song. This time that performer would be Brian Kennedy.

> It never occurred to me to take part in it. It was one of those things that, because I started off on the path of original music and went to London, it wasn't part of my world. It was a bit of fun representing your country. I never dreamed that one day RTÉ would approach me and ask if I wanted to represent my country and sing for Ireland. It was such an extraordinary curveball. There wasn't one reason against doing it. I never thought to submit a song for the Eurovision. The process has changed over the years. We used to go out to local songwriter competitions, then we got more savvy. It stopped being a local competition and the rules kept changing. I was living in London pursuing a solo career, working with Van Morrison. I had a few albums out by then. It was an incredible busy decade for me. It came out of the blue. I think RTÉ had been looking for an artist to represent them. I think they'd been looking at lots of footage. I had done a lot of television at the time and I think that people put their heads together. For some reason my name kept cropping up. It was quite a surprising offer. Beyond representing your country, there's not much left in the world to be proud of. It was something I knew I should consider very seriously and I did and I'm so glad that I did.

Once Brian accepted RTÉ's proposal, it was time to find the right song. Brian continues:

There were many, many songs submitted. I got to hear a bunch of them, it was done through a committee, comprised of Paul Brady, Juliet Turner and all people like that. By the time I had a meeting with all the songwriters, I said that I don't think any of the songs they showed me were strong enough to represent my country. I said, 'I don't feel like the ammunition is strong enough.' Every one of them turned to me and said, 'We're really glad you said that, because that's how we feel.' I know that Jimmy McCarthy had been in touch. They contacted him again, and he sent in his song 'The Greatest Song of All' and Don Mescal's song 'All Over The World'. I said, 'I have a song that might be appropriate, can I put it into the mix?' They said that I could, so I threw it in. It was 'Every Song is A Cry For Love'. We went to *The Late Late Show* and the people at home choose my song. I honestly didn't think that my song would get through. I thought they would go with Jimmy's or Don's. Don's song was up-tempo and had a gospel choir and Jimmy was such an established song writer.

Greece was the word for Brian, but first he had the obstacle of a semi-final to overcome. Brian was eighth on the night, performing the thousandth song at the Eurovision. Brian remembers Athens:

I'd never been to the Eurovision before, except for the interval act in Ireland. It was all new to me. By then it was a highly polished machine. The moment I stepped off the plane (a camera crew was constantly following me), I stopped being 'Brian Kennedy' and immediately became 'Ireland'. You immediately became a country. They would never say, 'Hi Brian'; I was constantly referred to as 'Ireland'. It was extra pressure performing in the semi-final, everything could have fallen down at that moment if we didn't get through. We were the tenth name out and by the time they got to the second last name we were looking at each other saying, 'Oh crap.' But they suddenly said 'Ireland', and it was like we'd won when we came last. It was a bit of a gamble as an established artist. It would have been very embarrassing if I hadn't gotten through to the final. We suddenly had to up our game and look at the production of the song and tighten up the performance any way we could. We were handed a new itinerary for the next day. There was never a moment to rest, and you suddenly go into final mode. You're being filmed all the time and they release those DVDs, so you're aware of being on camera the whole time. The semi-final is a bit of a dry-run, but the odd part is that the song is a little bit more familiar to everyone, so, yeah I think there are positives. I don't think they are the things that make you win but it comes down to the performance, how you perform it on that night with all that pressure, because you know the whole country is watching you, the whole world is watching you. I was very well aware that I had to do my absolute very best.

If Ireland was the last name to be called out in the semi, Iceland weren't so lucky. Brian recalls:

I remember in the semi-final that Iceland didn't get through. That girl went mental. She stormed the set and actually broke through security. She was so angry because she thought she deserved to win. She was like a little blonde Björk. Eventually she had to be escorted off the premises.

Ireland had qualified from a semi-final, thanks to Brian's talented team of brilliant musicians onstage with him that night. On guitar he had Calum McColl, and his backing vocalists were Fran King and Una Healy. Brian remembers Una:

I'll never forget when Una came to audition for us. She walked in with her guitar. She had a real musicality about her and was a lovely singer. We said 'Yes' straight away, and she became a huge star with The Saturdays.

On the night there was some serious Eurovision competition to contend with in the final. Brian was aware of most of it:

I was aware of Carola [the 1991 winner]. There was also a singer called Anna Vissi under the same pressure. She was like Madonna in that part of the world, a huge star. When she didn't do well they weren't happy. Some people were very friendly and some people were not friendly at all. To be honest, there is so little time to hang out with anybody, especially as some people have got a very kind of intricate performance and lots going on. There just isn't time to be sociable. There was a great deal of excitement when we all lined up.

Despite Brian thinking Bosnia should have won, it was Finland who claimed their first victory. He recalls the final well:

Where I go down on one knee during the song, which just happened naturally in rehearsals, I hadn't really planned for it. The verse is a little quieter and a little more intimate. We decided to keep it in as it would stand out from the other performances. Lordi had something that nobody else had. Everybody was talking about them. Even when they won and people asked me, 'How do you feel?' I said, 'Answer me one question, how does Lordi's song go? Sing it for me.' They couldn't – no one could. It wasn't about the song. It should really be about a catchy song. By the time we realised we could not win, we popped the champagne anyway and started to get drunk. It's very unpredictable who will win, and why.

Despite being unhappy with the winning song, Brian has no regrets about participating in the fifty-first Eurovision. He only has fond memories of a great time:

A lot of people hadn't heard of me before. It was the early days of the Internet, Facebook and Twitter. I was getting messages from all over the word saying that my song was the best and it should have won. It connected me to a network of people, people who are big Eurovision fans and run

Eurovision parties. I've been to a few over the years, and sang the song. For some of those people, it was their favourite song. When I was performing in the semi-final and final I had phone calls from Dana, Johnny Logan, Daniel O'Donnell and various people wishing me good luck, and saying, 'We're really proud of you.' It's lovely getting those messages. It's something that I will remember with great pride. It was great fun to be a part of. On the night of the Eurovision I usually go to Eurovision parties and it's made me a bigger fan.

CHAPTER NINE

FROM BUTCH TO LEANNE

Brian Kennedy's top-ten-place finish would be remembered for a long time. In the years following, Ireland struggled to get a foothold in the contest. Having missed the boat with 'The Voice', Dervish finally got their chance in 2007. That year, the Albanian backup jury saved Ireland the embarrassment of scoring a grand total of 'nul points'.

Ireland would reach an all-time low when we sent Dustin the Turkey to the event in 2008. Europe certainly didn't see the funny side, if there was one. Sinéad Mulvey and Black Daisy also failed to make the final, but Niamh Kavanagh restored some pride by reaching the final in Oslo with 'It's For You'.

As we moved into a new decade, one Irish woman would dominate the Eurovision. We had begun with Butch Moore, now it was time for Leanne Moore. Born in Limerick, Leanne's first memories of the Eurovision were jumping on the couch watching Linda and Niamh win for Ireland. The latter would become a personal favourite of Leanne, due to the fact it was the first Eurovision she watched after the death of her mother. In 2008, she won the TV show *You're A Star* and topped the Irish singles charts with 'On Wings'. In so doing, she and her mother had set a record. Her mother, Chris Moore, had a number one single in 1993. They are the only mother and daughter in Ireland to have achieved this.

Leanne participated in the 2010 Eurosong final and would be on the jury in 2014. She would go on to sing backing vocals for Ireland in three consecutive Eurovision finals. Ireland needed a new approach and Dublin twins Jedward would provide a breath of fresh air. They appealed to a younger audience. Dusseldorf was the first stop for Leanne in 2011:

Of the Eurovisions I went to, Dusseldorf was the most 'wow'. I loved everything about 'Lipstick'. Caroline [Downey] did an amazing job, from the staging to the rehearsal. Everything was so well prepared. I was so in love with the song, I thought it was amazing. I hadn't met Jedward before either and that was a whole thing in itself. It was incredible and I remember it like it was yesterday. When we were in Dusseldorf, even the backstage crew – the guys on the lighting and the guys handling our microphone stands – were all saying, 'We'll see you in Dublin next year.' I don't think we ever actually believed it would go that way. I remember thinking at the time how Jedward absolutely deserved it. I'd seen how hard they worked and how many times we'd gone over things and how good they were to people. They were never anything other than polite.

A year later Jedward were back again, this time in Azerbaijan, but lightning didn't strike twice. They qualified for the final with 'Waterline', but finished well down in the field. It was certainly a feeling of déjà vu for Leanne:

The whole crew that run it are the same people who travel around. You meet the same people working on sound and so on. That's what I didn't realise till I was there, that it's the same core group. It was like a little reunion. There were a couple of really cool acts on that year as well. The Russian Grannies were definitely a highlight. Loreen was staying in our hotel. She had so many backing singers and it was just incredible what they did. You would always hear them rehearsing in the hotel. She is mysterious in real life. She says very little. That was a stunning song. Songs like that are stand out winners.

While Jedward were performing at the Eurovision, one Irish promoter got the idea that perhaps a 'Best of Eurovision Winners' gig might be a good idea. Navan man Conor Mulhall got in contact with Louis Walsh. Conor rounded up all of Ireland's Eurovision winners for a short Irish tour. Eimear was pregnant at the time so couldn't commit to it, but Dana, Johnny, Linda, Niamh, Paul and Charlie agreed to it. Conor brought in Stuart O'Connor of Spotlight Productions and Eugene McCarthy directed an eight-piece band. The Sugar Cubes (which included Aileen Pringle who sang in the 1984 NSC) to put on a spectacular show. The opening night of the tour in Dublin was a treasure trove for Eurovision fans. Johnny Logan even performed 'Volare' and 'Euphoria'. He remembers that night well:

> I found it to be a very emotional night. I realised, that night, how much I had missed playing in Ireland and singing for my own people. It had been so many years that I'd been working away. On that night there was a particular feeling from the audience that was palpable, something you could touch. One of the other things I loved about that show was spending time with people like Charlie, Paul, Linda, Dana and all the rest of them. There was no internal jealousy or bickering, it was just lovely with all of us.

In 2013 Leanne was back, this time with Ryan Dolan in Malmö, the scene of Linda's greatest success. She linked up with the Irish team again. Linda recalls:

> A Swedish promoter brought me out. It had been twenty-one years since the first time. I went and asked him if he could book me into the same hotel as the Irish delegation as they're all buddies of mine, so that's what they did. Then RTÉ provided me with a ticket for the Eurovision. I saw the show, socialised and came home.

Malmö wouldn't prove as successful for the Irish the second time around. Leanne proved to be have some lucky Irish charm, qualifying from the semi-finals for the third consecutive year. We finished last of the twenty-six nations, but Leanne still loved the experience:

> Ryan's a fantastic singer, with the notes he can reach. I'd never been to Sweden. Linda came over and I said: 'Oh my

God Linda Martin's in Malmö.' she came over just to support everyone. She'd been with Stuart [O'Connor] who had done the staging that year. It was like a little Eurovision family. Malmö was my favourite destination. I just loved it and I've been back since with Liir and stayed in the same hotel. They're so healthy and fit and I'm mad about fitness and eating healthy. In Malmö they went overboard with everything, they just love the whole Eurovision experience. They really embrace it in Sweden, whereas in Ireland it gets a little bit lost. It was a massive disappointment afterwards. The voting that year was really at the centre of attention. I thought how it's going to be very difficult for Ireland to ever do well again. The song always speaks for itself. I think it should only be the countries that are in the final that should vote. I just found that on that night everyone was voting for neighbours and I'm not great at geography. Just like Jedward, we worked hard, and I don't think we deserved to come last.

Cork man Graham Norton showed his appreciation for the Irish team. Leanne recalls:

I was so excited. He came to find us afterwards. He'd been doing the commentary for the BBC and came to the dressing room. I was there bawling, I was so upset over it. He came in and said, 'Oh my Irish people.' It was just amazing. If I could meet himself and Ellen now I'd be so happy. He just walked into our dressing room and said 'You did very well,' and Ryan and took photos with us all. It was amazing.

We may not have seen the last of Leanne and her band, Liir. She's determined to get there again. Who better to ask why the Eurovision continues to be adored?:

Music just translates across every single culture, every nationality. Everybody understand music, everyone relates to it and no matter if there's a difference in the way Irish music has a Celtic element, whatever it is, it still is understandable. It's a way that for us to express who we are. Music makes people happy. It's one of those things that will keep on running and will have many faces in the future and will change over and over again. I don't think the Eurovision will ever, truly go away, and I don't think it ever should. When you look at the way that Australia got on board last year, you can see how it unites people from all around the world. That's what music is. If a person loves music, they're going to love the Eurovision.

Can-Linn featuring Kasey Smyth and Molly Sterling failing to qualify for the Eurovision final makes it four times in the last eight years that the Irish have been absent. It is without doubt our bleakest period in the contest's history. The RTÉ head of delegation, Michael Kealy, has received some negative press with regard to the Irish entries of recent years. Michael has done four Eurovisions so far. Along with the fifteenn to sixteen people in a delegation, he's in charge of the overall creative direction of the act: the consultation with the artist and making sure that they turn up for rehearsals. He is the first point of contact between the EBU and Ireland. Why does he think we're struggling?

The Eurovision is not the same contest it was fifty years ago. It's a completely different animal. There are forty odd countries instead of fifteen. Other countries pour millions into their entries. They have professional songwriters and professional performers. They have people who are used to performing on big stages. When we're not winning the contest, people tend to regard it as an amateur contest. Some of the songwriters who enter it are not professional songwriters. They're people who are accountants and postal workers by day and fancy their chances as a songwriter by night. It's the same as some of the performers. The performers are people who, generally speaking, haven't made it as professional performers. This doesn't apply to everyone, but it's like sending someone who's good at pitch'n'putt to go win the British Open. Then we're surprised when we don't do well. If you keep at it long enough, though, some good amateur songwriter will come up with a cracking song, and some singer that you have never heard of before will emerge. That's more of a hope than an expectation. In the rest of Europe, except for the UK and Ireland, there is no difference between the pop music business and the Eurovision. They are not mutually exclusive. You can be successful in the Eurovision and have a successful pop career. In the UK and Ireland they are seen as something separate. If you want to be seen as a serious pop star here, you don't enter the Eurovision because it's seen as an amateur competition, which it's not. It's enormous. There is a perception deficit here of the competition and that's one thing that we've been battling against. People who are serious about a career in music tend to not to want to enter the Eurovision.

The song that the Irish public vote for in the Eurosong final isn't necessarily the song that the Europeans are going fall in love with. Last year, Charlie McGettigan's song 'Anybody Got A Shoulder' won the jury vote, but was pipped on the final public vote. Does Michael Kealy think it's time to take it away from the public again?

We shouldn't necessarily trust the public's judgement on this sort of thing. It's great to consult the public on referendums as they always get it right, but consulting them on what is the best song for the Eurovision might not be the best thing to do. In fairness to Molly, she was a great performer and a great songwriter, but it was an enormous competition to send someone to. We're sending someone who is probably not used to performing in the parish hall to the biggest stage in the world. It's a huge ask. She did really well, but it was probably the wrong type of act to send. The public liked the idea of a sixteen-year-old songwriter. A lot of other countries don't consult the public vote when they send their acts. They have jury systems or select an act and send it without any consultation. The Austrians sent Conchita in 2014 and they didn't have a deciding competition. All of our seven winners were chosen without any reference to the public.

In 2015, about three hundred and twenty entries were received. Michael continues:

> There's a lot of 'have-a-go heroes' out there – people who
> are slightly delusional about their own talent and delusional
> about the nature of the Eurovision. A lot of people don't
> understand the sort of competition it is. It's not an amateur
> competition. It's like England winning the World Cup in '66.
> They invented the game and they think they own it, so
> they're always disappointed if they don't get to the final.
> We're the same with the Eurovision. We think we invented
> it because we've won it seven times and when other people
> are better than us we still feel entitled to be in the top ten.
> The problem is that the calibre of the people enteringsongs
> sometimes just isn't great. It's not as if we don't want to win
> it. We're trying to send the best of what we've got. I'm sure
> plenty of people would like to see me dragged out and hung
> from the mast in RTÉ because of my track record with the
> Eurovision. Do I enjoy doing it? Of course I do. Whether I
> do it again is a question for other people.

In 2016, Ireland is sending its fiftieth song to the event. It's twenty years since Ireland last won the event. Those who have been there can surely provide the template for the years ahead. People such as Bill Whelan offer fascinating and knowledgeable opinions:

> At the end of the day, it does come down to the song. No-
> body has approached this issue. We've done badly because
> we've done everything, even Dustin the Turkey. We've been
> absurd and cynical about the Eurovision. The reason we
> don't succeed is because when we were winning it, we en-
> tered it without cynicism. The turkey was a smart alec move.
> We've done worse and worse because we're forgetting what
> will actually win it on the night. You might get weirdos win-
> ning it occasionally, but I believe that a good song will win
> it.

Johnny Logan agrees that it's all about the song:

> We should stop thinking about winning and start thinking about sending a song that represents the country. All of these attempts to use social media to win the contest are wrong. It should be the song that wins rather than a popularity contest.

Brendan Graham may not be finished yet. He has this to say:

> It's totally about the song and that should never ever be forgotten. It has to be catchy, have a nice idea and, of course, have the right performer. We have performers on every station in the country. It's about getting the song right, so that people will come through when the time is right. I wouldn't change our approach to music. In this country it has always been rooted to the land, with a tradition of beautiful melodies. There might be a young budding male or female songwriter somewhere around the country wanting to enter. We have the source, we have the deep well here in this country and that's what we should be concentrating on. I haven't entered since. I felt a sense of honour when we were representing the country and we had certain success. I loved the people who I was working with. There is a small part of me that says no one has ever won it three times.

Phil Coulter offers some solid advice to aspiring songwriters:

> The song has to have a certain charm about it. It must have that every second counts quality. You can't waste eight bars. This is the sort of stuff that is second nature to guys like me. An aspiring amateur songwriter needs to get that. It has to reach out to the people of Azerbaijan and Turkey and so on. It has got to have something that is different, a hook that makes it stand out from the crowd. To begin with, you need the song to begin with, then you need the performer and then you need the presentation. It's not that this coun-

try doesn't have talented songwriters, singers or choreographers and visualisers or people who have mastered all that technology. It's not that we don't have that, it's just that we need to learn how to harness that ability, and persuade them that the Eurovision is worth doing.

Louis Walsh says it like it is:

> We're sending these forgettable songs without a hook. It has to be catchy, either rock 'n' roll or a ballad, like Johnny or Linda or Niamh. If RTÉ were reallyserious about it, someone in there would just say, 'I'm going to get a great song and a great band.' Amateurs will never win it – they'll never have the longevity that Linda and Johnny have. You need the professionals, someone that's out there doing it, not afraid to go out on that stage and give a good performance.

As we look forward, I have no doubt that the Eurovision Song Contest will still be there in 2056, to celebrate its centenary. Ireland will hopefully still be participating. Why has it lasted so long? The final word goes to Linda:

> It makes a lot of money for a lot of people. That's why it has survived. It's the biggest song contest in the world. It has about two hundred million people watching a television show. It's fun. Regardless of the critics and regardless of who sneers at it, it's meant to be a night of fun, a night of entertainment. It's not the Nobel Peace Prize and it's not going to change the world. You just watch it, have a laugh, have a party, dress up and do whatever you're going to do. If Ireland win, brilliant. If they don't, well, as Johnny would say 'What's Another Year?'

CHAPTER TEN

NOEL KELEHAN REMEMBERED

Over the course of this book, we have heard from most of Irish people who have been involved in the contest. Johnny Logan, Brendan Graham and Phil Coulter may be our most successful songwriters in the history of the Eurovision and Bill Whelan has produced three winning songs and written two interval pieces, but there is one person who, without doubt, is the most distinguished Irish person ever associated with the NSC and Eurovision.

Noel Kelehan was born in Dublin on St Stephen's Day in 1935. He learnt to play the piano at an early age and started a career in music during his teenage years. In the early 1960s Noel became the musical director for *The Late Late Show*. Even the songwriters of Butch Moore's Eurovision entry didn't go to Naples in 1965, so Luxembourg in '66 was Noel's first Eurovision. In the late sixties he had his own trio that played the Shelbourne Hotel. It made more sense financially for him to stay in Dublin the week Dana participated than attend the contest in Amsterdam since RTÉ wouldn't pay him what he requested.

He composed the opening theme music for the Eurovision in Dublin in 1971, even though Colman Pearce was the musical director. Noel continued to be associated with the Eurovision throughout the late seventies and was there in The Hague when 'What's Another Year' won in 1980.

Again, Noel composed the opening piece of music for the RDS contest in 1981and became friends with several of the other conductors, including BBC conductor Ronnie Hazlehurst. Away from Eurovision, most notably, Noel arranged the strings on U2's song 'The Unforgettable Fire' in the mid '80s. In Zagreb 1990,

Yugoslav TV didn't want to show the conductors taking their bow beforehand but Noel took leadership when the conductors threatened to strike and the decision was reversed. Noel's bow wasn't transmitted though, either because he was the ringleader or because the song didn't commence with the orchestra.

In total, Noel conducted twenty-four Irish entries in the thirty-two years that he was involved with the Eurovision. He was chief conductor for the Eurovisions in Ireland in 1981, 1988, 1993, 1994 and 1995 and also conducted entries for Bosnia, Romania, Greece and Poland over the years. He led the orchestra on twenty-nine entries and led the RTÉ Concert Orchestra for twenty-seven Irish national finals between 1965 and 1996. Nobody took part in the Eurovision Song Contest more than Noel did.

His favourite Eurovision winner was 'In Your Eyes' by Niamh Kavanagh and 1998 was the final year the orchestra was used in Eurovision. Noel retired in 2000 and later developed Alzheimer's. He died in February 2012 and at his funeral mass Eimear Quinn sang 'Be Not Afraid' and *'Ave Maria'*, while the orchestra also played Noel's arrangement to 'Send in the Clowns.' Everybody who worked with Neol had similar comments to say and I thought it only appropriate to include a selection of them here.

> Noel Kelehan was a most amenable chap. He was the official accompanist of *The Late Late Show* at that time, we had an old upright piano and he sat in the corner. If anybody in the audience wanted to sing a song, Noel had to accompany them and find out what key they were in and all that usual ballyhoo. He was a most pleasant, easy-going, lovely, charming guy and an outstanding musician. I only have the fondest, fondest memories of him. He later took up the job of conducting the Irish entry in the Eurovision and he was widely respected for that. He just became part of the furniture, when you were looking at the Eurovision and looking at the National Song Contest you expected Noel Kelehan to be there, like it wasn't complete unless he was, and he was a lovely guy. Everyone will say the same.
>
> –Gay Byrne

Noel Kelehan, God rest him, always had the orchestra on his side. No matter what country the Eurovision was being held in, all the musicians knew Noel and he knew a good few of them. I remember them all clapping their hands and saying: 'Where's the Jazz session tonight, Noel? When we get all of this out of the way?' and it just gave the performer a very comfortable feeling with the musicians because they loved Noel.

–Linda Martin

He was a great jazz musician. I spent a week with him in Belgium with Honor Heffernan about thirty years ago. He was such fun. He has a story for every day of his life.

–Charlie McGettigan

Noel Kelehan was a great character and a great musician. He'd always have a fag dangling out of the side of his mouth. He was a gem - a lovely bloke.

–Shay Healy

He was an incredible man; He wasn't just an incredible musician and conductor, he was a very charming man. I always wanted to meet him again.

–Muriel Day

Noel Kelehan is someone who I adore. Noel was Eurovision Ireland, really. He was responsible for the orchestra, for all the in and outs, the beginnings and the ends. He was just wonderful to be with. I have a treasured photograph of Noel and myself in Millstreet.

–Fionnuala Sherry

Noel was the ultimate professional musician. He was jazz at heart. The orchestra had an immense respect for him because Noel could just silence the room or make the room laugh and I'm talking a forty piece orchestra. There was a deep respect there and he was a great man for the harmonies as well and he was a stabbing piano player. I had the honour of working with him many, many times. When I competed in the Eurovision Anniversary concert in the National Concert Hall. In the last five years, I actually wrote a piece to Noel, to dedicate it to him (because he had just passed), to say we cannot ever forget the contribution that man made. His wife was in the audience and I didn't know and she was so, so thankful because Noel was going to every Eurovision, therefore he was representing Ireland. Noel would be the quiet ambassador for decades of Ireland at the Eurovision. The conductors from other countries would come over and ask: 'Where's Noel? Where's Noel?' He was so well known and respected by the viewers and musicians. I feel very proud to have known him.

–Maxi

I met Noel Kelehan many, many times. An absolute-gentleman. He was the perfect gentleman; there was no doubt about it.

–Marc Roberts

A gentleman and a funny man, a gifted man, and for me, as a young musician coming in, Noel was a tremendous support. I was like a fish out of water, I didn't know anyone in RTÉ as a young freelance musician and I was doing early arrangements with the orchestra. The earliest things I would have arranged, Noel conducted them and he always had something helpful to say. I will never forget him for his encouragement because he was older and very well experienced. A wonderful arranger. He was a great friend and one of the best story-tellers of all time. He enjoyed the Eurovision. He was a very influential person.

–Bill Whelan

I remember doing a show with Noel for the Benevolent Society in RTÉ. I went up to his house for rehearsal and I remember doing 'Let There Be Love' with Noel's piano playing and I rehearsed it with him. In the end I did the show but Noel was great. He played for me loads of times, a great piano player. He went to the movies with Dickie and myself. We all loved cowboy movies and westerns.

–Rowland Soper

I remember doing a tribute to Noel Kelehan with the orchestra and Charlie and I actually performed 'Rock 'n' Roll Kids' for the first time with an orchestra at his retirement. It was hosted by Mike Murphy and it was a lovely evening. I remember being with my brother Robert and my mother, both deceased now. In fact I'm the only one who's alive. The table had my brother, my mother and Ronnie Drew. Oh, and Charlie was at the table. I forgot about Charlie. He's still alive [laughs].

–Paul Harrington

I only knew Noel just through Eurovision and at a few concerts afterwards. I sang at his funeral. He was amazingly talented.

–Eimear Quinn

He was a lovely guy and a brilliant jazz pianist. He would have been part of the fixtures and fittings in RTÉ as the conductor. A very charming and able fella and very likeable. He would have been part of the RTÉ landscape, in the days when there was the orchestra, there was always Noel.

–Phil Coulter

I've huge memories obviously, because I played with the Noel Kelehan Trio, The Noel Kelehan Quintet and the Noel Kelehan Big Band. There were two drummers involved in jazz Dublin in those days and Noel Kelehan literally chose me as his drummer. I soldiered with Noel for quite a few years and we played in the Shelbourne Hotel restaurant a few nights every week, so I would hold Noel in the highest esteem. Simply playing with him, he didn't have to be a teacher, but he taught you how to play modern jazz and then I worked with Noel as a conductor on many a music show we did over the years, from Sandy Kelly and all the various shows RTÉ did over the years, Noel would have been conductor. Totally talented, ooh, what a player. Easily our foremost jazz pianist.

–Ian McGarry

I knew Noel very well. He was a staff man in RTÉ with the Light Orchestra. He was a lovely fella. He conducted for other countries as well when they didn't have a conductor. I think he was very disappointed when they did away with the orchestra.

–Larry Gogan

When I did 'The Likes of Mike' for the 'Mike Murphy Show', I was the singer on it for the twelve weeks or however long it ran, Noel did all the music and arrangements for the show. I worked with him all the time. He was just a gentleman. Such a funny man and a great prankster. The Eurovision wasn't the Eurovision until you'd see Noel getting up on the podium and here was Ireland's entry. I think he was better known than anybody for conducting the orchestra. He was the Eurovision.

–Alma Carroll

I can't think of the Eurovision without thinking of Noel. When you went out on that stage, you felt so totally alone and you looked over and you saw Noel standing on the podium and he'd just wink at you. Then you knew everything was going to be OK because you knew already that you had every musician in the pit on your side.

–Johnny Logan